# Horse-friendly
# RIDING

# Horse-friendly
# RIDING

Schooling that puts the horse first

## SUSAN McBANE

J. A. ALLEN

*To my next horse, whoever he or she may be.*

© *Susan McBane 2009*
*First published in Great Britain 2009*

ISBN 978 0 85131 957 5

J.A. Allen
Clerkenwell House
Clerkenwell Green
London EC1R 0HT

J.A. Allen is an imprint of Robert Hale Ltd

www.halebooks.com

The right of Susan McBane to be identified as author
of this work has been asserted by her in accordance
with the Copyright, Designs and Patents Act 1988

*British Library Cataloguing in Publication Data*
A catalogue record for this book is available from the British Library

Photographs by Sally and David Waters, except for the two on page 141, courtesy of Sarah Fisher and the one on page 148 reproduced from Reiner Klimke's *Basic Training of the Young Horse*. Illustrations on page 98 by Dianne Breeze.

Edited by Martin Diggle
Design by Judy Linard
Printed by Kyodo Nation Printing Services Co. Ltd, Thailand

# Contents

Acknowledgements 9

Horse-friendly Priorities 11

1. What Horses Can and Cannot Do 15
   The Horse's Strong Points 16
   Characteristics That Can Prove Challenging to Humans 19
      The Horse's Senses
   Conformation and Action 23
      Basic Symmetry
      Specific Points
      The Horse in Action
      Qualities of Gaits
   The Job for the Horse 41
   Working with the Horse's Mind 42
      The Horse's Capacity for Learning
      Reasoning Power
      Concentration
   Body Language and Behaviour 48
      A Physical Language

2. At What Age Should You Start? 52
   A Training Schedule 54
      The Day after Birth Onwards
      Weaning
      Yearlings
      Two-year-olds
      Three-year-olds

Four-year-olds
Five-years-olds
Other Progressions     59
    Starting Young
    Leaving it Late

3.   The Effect of the Herd     61
    How Horses Learn in Their Natural State     61
      Natural Parameters
    Learning to Interact with Humans     63
      Horse Don't Forget, but can Relearn
      Pressure
      From Ground to Saddle

4.   The Rider's Responsibility     72
    Attitude     73
    Technique     75
    Horsemanship     75
    Equine Personalities     76
      Reticent
      Timid
      Domineering
      Lazy
      Keen
      Not Co-operative
      Willing
      Confident
    Trust     80

5.   The Aids     82
    How We Send Signals     84
      The Voice
      Body Posture
      The Legs
      The Reins and Bit
      Combining Weight Aids with Other Aids
    Mental/Visual Communication     106
      Breathing as an Aid
    Artificial Aids     107
      Whips

Spurs  
Timing, Reward and Correction             109

6.   Tack                          111  
    Saddles                  112  
        Basic Rules of Fitting  
        Types and Designs  
        Numnahs and Pads  
        Girths  
        Stirrups  
        Thoughts on Saddling  
    Bridles                   120  
        Basic Points of Fitting a Bridle  
    Bits                     123  
        The Correct Fitting of Bits  
        Bitless Bridles  
    Training Aids           127

7.   Groundwork            130  
    Groundwork as an Aid to Riding    131  
    Long-reining            132  
        Equipment for Long-reining  
        Basic Long-reining Procedure  
    Lungeing              135  
        Equipment for Lungeing  
        Basic Lungeing Procedure  
    Tellington Touch Equine Awareness Method (TTEAM)    140  
    Loose Schooling         141

8.   The Forward Ethic       144  
    What does 'Forward' Mean?      144  
    The Background to Forwardness    145  
    Instilling Forwardness       146  
    Exceptional Circumstances     147

9.   Riding from Back to Front    150  
    The Skeleton and Spinal Movement   151  
    Muscles and Tendons       152  
        Rest and Relaxation  
        The 'Ring of Muscles'

Engagement     155
    Working Long-and-low
    Working the More Advanced Horse
Impulsion     163
    How to Ask for Impulsion
Collection     166

10. Calm, Forward and Straight     168
Calmness     168
    How to Achieve Calmness
Forwardness     171
    Balance
    Rhythm
Straightness     174
    Assessing Horse and Rider for Straightness
    Straightening the Crooked Horse

11. What to Teach When     178
Suggested Schooling Sequence under Saddle     180
Pole Work and Jumping     181
    Approximate Distances between Poles
    Small Jumps
    Grid Work
Hacking     185

12. When Things go Wrong     187
Some Common Problems     188
    Inherited Problems
    Newly Apparent Problems
    Problems of Management
Maintaining Your Horse's Spirit     194

Further Reading     195

Index     197

# Acknowledgements

I wish to thank Sally and David Waters for undertaking to supply photographs for this book at a time when they were excessively busy with other projects. Illustrations are so important to a book like this and, despite being under stress, they have produced pictures of their usual top standard, for which I am most grateful. Sarah Fisher and Dianne Breeze also helped out by supplying illustrations and my thanks go to them as well.

I'd also like to thank my friends Anne Wilson and Pauline Finch for acting as sounding boards for my frequent queries, theories and ideas, and my eagle-eyed, ever-tactful copy editor on the Allen team, Martin Diggle, all of whom have given much thought-provoking, balancing input.

Finally, Cassandra Campbell, J.A. Allen's Commissioning Editor at Robert Hale, and Lesley Gowers, who took over from her, have both been understanding, encouraging and patient in bringing the book together with such a light touch and master-minding it through to completion. I hope it lives up to their expectations and the Allen reputation.

# Horse-friendly Priorities

This is a look at riding largely from the horse's point of view. Although some of the actual techniques and practicalities of riding will be explained and described, readers will find more details on actually how to ride in the books listed in Further Reading towards the end of this text. To provide a link with some of the ideas discussed in these pages, a few of the books in that list are my own, but most, both old and new, are by other authors. These have all helped me greatly, not only from the angle of learning about different riding techniques but also as confirmation of what I was taught about horses, my attitude towards them and how I feel naturally about them. I recommend all these books to readers of this one as means of promoting learning, a 'thinking' attitude, an inquiring mind, a critical orientation and, probably most important of all, the development of that fundamental, essential personal policy, not so evident today, of *putting the horse first*.

Most people who care a good deal for their horses would hate to think that the way they rode caused them discomfort, confusion or even pain and distress. Such owners and riders, as well as wanting to enjoy themselves, will try to ride both effectively and in a way which gives them the results they want, but which their horses understand and find comfortable and, they hope, is enjoyable for them, too.

They may have lessons, read books, watch DVDs and videos, go to lecture-demonstrations and attend courses, all with a view to increasing their knowledge, improving their techniques and generally becoming the best riders they can be. It can't have escaped their notice that there are plenty of conflicting views out there; different advice from equally impressive 'names' and from one teacher to another, at all levels. Other horse-owners and maybe livery yard proprietors will offer yet more contrary advice and it can all become thoroughly overwhelming. They end up not knowing who to believe, what to do or what is right and wrong.

As a teacher, I have found very often that new clients use techniques and follow policies which are clearly upsetting to their horses, which cause them discomfort or even pain, which are difficult for them to comply with and which cannot be called horse-friendly. Sadly, and quite possibly owing to the pressures of the competition sector of the horse world (not only competing itself, but also producing horses and ponies for competition), the riding and schooling methods which filter out to the rest of the horse world, and so are in general use today, are often brow-beating, forceful and confrontational, but many 'ordinary' riders genuinely do not realize this. They usually think that they must be correct – 'the thing to do' – either because an instructor has told them to do … (whatever it is), because 'everyone does it', or because they have seen some well-known or successful competition rider doing it.

All these are understandable if rather woolly reasons for riding in certain not very horse-friendly ways. While the method(s) used may sometimes produce winning results, these will be at the expense of the horse's spirit and enjoyment, his short-term contentment and his long-term welfare and well-being. I ask readers to consider the fact that, just because a horse wins prizes or transfers kudos to his connections in some other way, it does not always follow, by any means, that he has been managed, schooled, produced and ridden in a particularly horse-friendly way.

Some judges nowadays are, themselves, the product of this pushy and over-ambitious way of going on with horses, so they are propagating it amongst those who present themselves before them for judging. Competitors who win prizes under such conditions are likely to go on doing whatever they think the judge likes.

*The most important source to consult as to whether or not a technique or policy is horse-friendly is the horse himself. Just look at the horse and watch him very closely, not only when he is working.* This means ignoring:

- Who his rider and other connections are (no matter how famous).
- What establishment he comes from (no matter how impressive).
- What he has won (no matter how prestigious).
- What other horses he has beaten (which is of no importance to the horse).
- The circumstances or situation in which he is being kept or ridden (the location, the occasion or the purpose).
- What anyone near you is saying (no matter who they are).

To understand the horse's 'reply', you do need at least a sound, basic, working knowledge of equine 'body language' and behaviour and I present this towards the end of Chapter 1. Returning to the Further Reading, you will find excellent books on these topics listed there, as well, so I hope that you will continue along this crucial line via them.

Our aims, if we want to achieve horse-friendly riding, must be:

1. To use techniques and follow policies which will not cause discomfort and distress to our horses (commensurate with producing a compliant, safe horse).
2. To use techniques and follow policies which comprise rational methods of schooling and riding (which horses can understand because they comply with how they think and learn, and with which they can physically comply quite comfortably because they accord with how their bodies are constructed and how they function).
3. To give them plenty of time to grow and develop mentally and physically, to become strong and athletically fit enough for the work we require (which itself can help to make them fit), to recover from any illness and injury and to absorb and familiarize themselves with their lessons and experiences.
4. To manage and care for them in ways which are best for the equine body, mind and spirit – whether or not they accord with our own desires and requirements.
5. Most importantly, always to put the welfare and well-being of our horses before our own wants or ambitions.

These are not lofty aims, but accessible and ethically founded principles which will ultimately produce far, far better results than lower standards. Riding in a horse-friendly way does not mean being weak, indecisive or ineffectual. It does not mean allowing a horse always to have his own way, or never making any (reasonable) demands upon him. It means riding him in a way which does not distress him, which he understands, which he is not frightened of or confused by and which he is happy with, confident about and actually enjoys.

It means, also, riding him in such a way as to develop his body so that he himself develops the strength and agility to work safely under our weight, and to develop his mind so that he knows he is one of a pair in a mutually respectful partnership. This kind of riding enriches the lives of both horse and rider.

# CHAPTER 1

# What Horses Can and Cannot Do

Humans have been attracted to horses for thousands of years. At first they treated horses as a food source or farm animal, then as a means of transport and a tool for war. Then, as man had more and more to do with horses and learned more about how to breed, manage, train and use them, increasing use as a sporting vehicle became evident. Amongst certain cultures, and in many individual cases, a friendly and companionable relationship developed between man and horse.

Horses developed the mental and physical qualities they possess over many millennia in the hard school of surviving in the wild as prey animals. They have a combination of qualities which no other animal has, which makes them unique in the animal kingdom. The horse's good qualities have made him well-nigh indispensable to us over the years. Even now, when horses are, in the Western world, not essential for war and transport, life without them seems unimaginable to many people. It is not only riders who feel this way; many people own or mix with horses just because they want to be around them.

But there's a catch: horses' qualities include some which can make dealing with them difficult for the unwary or the uninformed. In short, their characteristics can be a two-edged sword. You have to deal with all aspects of horses' natural and instinctive behaviour if you want to be successful with them. I'm not talking here about success in terms of winning in competition, but about the more complex scenario of how horses behave well and thrive in body, mind and spirit under the management of some people but become 'problem horses' and thoroughly deprived and miserable under the management of others.

## THE HORSE'S STRONG POINTS

The general characteristics which attract us to horses are their size, strength, speed, stamina, sensitivity, intelligence (a moot point, discussed later), sociability and adaptability. No other animal combines all these factors in one body. Added to these is the conveniently formed equine back – ideal for sitting on, especially with the help of a saddle – and also the athleticism and jumping ability of some horses.

The saying 'as strong as a horse' did not arise without foundation. Even small ponies can carry and pull amazing weights with apparent ease (which is no reason to overload them, of course). It is well known that a strong, well-made pony or a cob can carry more weight for his size than a horse. This means that horses were soon seen as ideal (with some training) for pulling carts, chariots, farm vehicles and machinery, coaches and carriages, and for riding for a whole variety of purposes covered, in broad terms, by transport, war and sport.

The relative weight-carrying abilities of different types/breeds notwith-standing, a horse-friendly rider will try to 'ride light', as we say. This does not imply crouching or hovering 'above' the saddle, but sitting in as still and balanced a position as possible (without using the reins to maintain that balance). This not only minimizes the rider's impact on the horse's balance and movement, but also makes it easier to apply accurate aids of the right intensity at the right moment.

The horse's sensitivity (through the neural pathways) makes it possible for a good rider to use the lightest aids of rein, legs, seat/weight and position. When handling horses, it only takes a slight touch to get a horse to move over in the stable. (However, this sensitivity is also evidenced by horses' distress when exposed to the attacks of insects and, once we have understood and accepted how sensitive horses are, and how frightening pain is to them, it must make us wonder how some people can so readily thrash them as they do.)

The horse's mouth, like our own, is one of his most sensitive parts and it continues to be a subject of debate amongst both scientists and lay people, professional and amateur riders, as to why so many horses push against (or 'lean on') the bit with apparent equanimity. Continued, unrelieved, firm pressure (contact) such as many riders use does not make for lightness or balance in the horse and is unfair to him. Rough use of the bit (or any other kind of rough usage) is, of course, abuse and

Man's breeding efforts have produced vastly different types of equines from small children's ponies to massive heavy horses. This substantial, native type of pony is being ridden kindly and looks willing and interested in his work. Ponies like this have historically carried much heavier burdens than this young rider.

therefore strictly speaking unlawful, and can permanently damage the mouth.

It should always be a guiding principle that we use the lightest aids we possibly can which will produce the desired result. This applies to both legs and hands. The main reasons why a horse might resist the aids are that:

- He does not understand them.
- He has not been schooled to respond quickly and reliably.
- He does not want to comply.
- They are causing him discomfort or pain.
- He knows or is afraid that he cannot do what is being requested, or demanded.
- He is afraid that complying will be very uncomfortable.

It is not that the horse cannot *feel* the aids. Many riders are so busy or careless with their bodies in the saddle that horses can have a problem distinguishing whether or not a movement is just 'white noise' or actually means 'do something'. Such horses often need quite firm, exaggerated aids in order to produce a response. This, of course, is the rider's fault, not that of the horse.

Horses are amongst the fastest land animals on the planet: as prey animals,

Many of us tend to underestimate the effects of the horse's innate survival mechanism, and to overlook the fact that his senses give him a rather different perception of the world from ours. Horses can become startled or 'nappy' at almost anything that worries or frightens them. Behaviour which appears uncooperative can, understandably, also be caused by discomfort and pain caused by poor riding and/or uncomfortable or ill-fitting tack, or even the expectation or memory of them.

their speed is what keeps them alive, provided they start running soon enough after they recognize that a predator is in hunting mode. From our point of view, speed is an invaluable trait which has won battles and races, delivered messages in double-quick time, got us where we've wanted to go faster than any other method before cars were invented and given us lots of fun and exhilaration – and undoubtedly sometimes terrified us as well.

Very roughly, Thoroughbred horses can run at around 40 mph (64 kph) flat out and have the stamina to outlast feline predators – but not canines. This combination of speed and stamina with strength has made horses more useful for various tasks than any other animal. On top of that is their amazing adaptability to changing circumstances and their 'trainability' provided they are trained in a way which their brains can understand. The Babylonians had a go at breaking in and training onagers, but onagers do not have the horse's other priceless quality – sociability – so the Babylonians apparently gave up relatively quickly, probably fed up with being gratuitously bitten, kicked and resisted.

Going back to horses' brains, it is true that they are small for the size of the animal they control. Horses are mammals, of course, and their brains function pretty much like ours, but they lack the part of the brain responsible for higher mental functions (present only in humans, the great apes, dolphins and whales) like logic and rationality. Some people say that horses are not capable of feeling emotions, but this is patently untrue! Quite a lot of people, both scientists and others, say that horses are not intelligent and do not come high on the list of the world's intelligent animals. The point is that their brains equip them brilliantly *for the life they evolved to live* but the amazing thing is that those brains are capable of *adapting* to a life with humans (sociability

Some experts think that the horse's distant ancestors who lived in swampy forests developed natural jumping skills – jumping over fallen tree trunks and a forest floor littered with obstacles – and that this trait has come down to modern horses. This could certainly be a reason why some horses like jumping and are good at it but others are not.

coming in here) and learning all the things which we want of horses. They learn much more quickly and effectively if we train them in a way which accords with how their brains function, horses learning by the association of ideas and the formation of habits – which they do very quickly.

We must mention the horse's ability to jump, of course. Many people believe that horses are not natural jumpers because the environment in which they evolved most recently in their development was open, grassy plains. Further back in time, though, the modern horse's ancestors were forest and swamp dwellers and would have developed the ability to jump over obstacles such as fallen trees, or streams. Many horses and ponies are not only very good at jumping but clearly enjoy it. Some aren't and don't. But the speed and strength all horses possess, combined with the traits of enjoying jumping and having the ability for it, have enhanced enormously the popularity of horses with humans.

## CHARACTERISTICS THAT CAN PROVE CHALLENGING TO HUMANS

Of course, with all the advantages offered to humans by horses there has to be a downside and there are several from our point of view.

A prey animal needs a brilliant memory: it has been said that, never mind elephants, horses never forget, either. As a prey animal living in open country, the horse needs a one-take ability to make mental maps. Horses seem to remember for life the places they have been to, even if only once. They also remember acutely what happened or happens to them there, and it only takes one good or bad incident to form a memory. Once something awful has happened to a horse in a particular place he will always remember it, even though nothing but good has happened before or since. Since horses are individuals, they do vary in how they respond to their life incidents. Some horses, after a bad experience in a particular place, will react in a defensive way in future whenever they go there, but others will not. (It is amazing that some equines may, after experiencing a terrifying accident in transit, load up and travel again afterwards as though it had never happened.) It is usually possible to erase or 'overlay' bad memories and get horses to associate the place once more with good things, or to learn, for instance, that not all yellow tractors or high vehicles are dangerous, but it has to be done correctly by a confident, fairly fearless rider who is acutely attuned to the horse's responses and motivated to restore his confidence.

From the point of view of being ridden generally, if a horse forms a reliable association with riding and pain/discomfort, he will naturally behave defensively under saddle and, as with anything performed regularly, this can remain a habit even under a new and better rider. The habit can be pushed well into the background during re-schooling and rehabilitation, but it will recur if the circumstances which caused it (such as a bad rider who is whip-happy, kicks hard wearing spurs, or pulls or stabs at the bit) arise again.

The horse's instinctive tendency to react first to something alarming or suspicious and think (maybe) later is essential to his survival as a prey animal. In fact, we do it ourselves. If something near us makes a loud noise or sudden movement we jump – although we don't normally take to our heels and run away as fast as we can. This, however, is the horse's instinct because sudden noises and movements nearby mean danger (a predator) in his evolutionary 'memory'. He is hard-wired, programmed, to respond in this way to escape as fast as possible. This means that quiet, steady, calm people always do better with horses than the more hyper sort – those who shout, behave roughly, treat horses brusquely, move quickly, are noisy with voice and equipment and so on. Nervous people often put horses on edge in a similar way because the horse evolved to sense nervousness in his herd-mates and treat it as a warning of danger.

## *The Horse's Senses*

The horse's five senses – hearing, sight, smell, taste and touch – give him a different perception of the world from ours and this can cause difficulties for us if we simply do not understand what is happening.

### HEARING

The horse's hearing is more acute than ours and he can hear higher-pitched sounds which we cannot hear at all. This can account for apparently strange or spooky behaviour as he listens to something we are unaware of.

### EYESIGHT

The horse's eyesight is quite different from ours. His overall *field* of vision is much wider than a person's, which means he may see, and react to, things beyond the periphery of his rider's vision, but his *depth* of vision seems to be much less developed than a human's. It is vital for us to adapt to these differences during riding if we want the horse to see well and clearly enough to be safe to ride, and to perform effectively. For example, since a horse cannot adjust the lenses of his eyes to focus as we do, when jumping, he must move his head into such a position that the image of the fence falls on to part of his eye called 'the visual streak'. This is a narrow band enabling fairly clear vision which runs across the back of his eye, on the retina on to which all images are projected. We can't expect him to go with the desired free, forward movement (including the act of jumping) if he can't see clearly, and he cannot focus without the free use of his head and neck without looking upwards uncomfortably with just his eyes.

### SMELL

This may not appear immediately to have anything to do with riding, but it can be a cause of distraction or uncertain behaviour if the horse smells something we cannot – and the horse's sense of smell is almost as acute as that of dogs. A particular scent can bring flying back to us the memory of a particular event, person or place and I am sure that this happens with horses too, since they learn naturally by association of ideas. So, this is something which can affect the horse when we are riding. His behaviour at the memory evoked may be incomprehensible to us – and quite possibly something we do not want. It also seems possible that horses can react 'at first instance' to smells they dislike/mistrust ('smells nasty – might be dangerous').

## TASTE

This is a sense we can use to our advantage when giving food rewards and we can create a pleasant association with something which might otherwise be worrying or unpleasant for the horse, such as veterinary attention or farriery, by giving him his favourite titbits during the procedure. This has been shown to create a pleasant association with a tricky situation and improve the horse's behaviour. If we can use a food reward quickly enough (within a second or two at the most) of his obeying a command or aid, for instance, he can associate the two – although this is very difficult to do when in the saddle.

Taste is also involved in the wide range of flavoured bits which are on the market now. I personally do not believe the sales pitch which states that they create a pleasant taste in the horse's mouth which makes him salivate and keep the mouth soft – although I daresay that those marketing these bits believe this. A vet once told me that some metals actually cause a mild irritation in the mouth, which could well cause salivation, but I certainly would not want this for my horse. This vet also confirmed to me, a long time ago, that excessive salivation (frothing and drooling) is a sign of distress in mammals and not something we should be happy about. This is something widely misunderstood among riders: we should aim for a *moist* mouth, definitely not 'the more froth the better'. However, it does seem to be the case that some individuals naturally produce rather more saliva than others.

If a horse does not like the taste of his bit, he may show it by excessive champing and mouthing, trying to get away from it. An old mare showed clearly that she hated the rubber bit I had bought (and thoroughly washed) for her by standing with her head vertical to the ground and her mouth wide open, with a distressed look in her eye, so I changed it at once for tasteless stainless steel.

I believe it fairer to the horse to use a bit which is tasteless and to give a mint or whatever the horse likes when it is put in: that way, the good taste will linger and you can be sure that he does not have in his mouth a taste he dislikes.

TOUCH

This sense is, of course, used a lot when riding. We know that horses are very sensitive and that we should use the lightest aids we can which will get the desired result. Problems arise when heavier and heavier aids are applied to get a horse to respond when, as mentioned earlier, there is a very good reason why he cannot do so. This sense is abused when spurs (particularly the type capable of damaging the skin) are used strongly, when bits are used harshly, when the horse is ridden on a more or less permanent and firm contact (guaranteed to dull the mouth) and when riders use the whip to flog or thrash a horse rather than for direction and information – or as a moderate reminder if this is genuinely justified.

It is not only the horse's mouth which can be dulled by unremitting contact. The horse's sides can also become dulled by the form of riding in which the rider's legs are kept pressed against the horse's sides instead of being just draped around them like a wet towel. Horses who are not light in the mouth and sides are not pleasant to ride but, with correct schooling, this tendency can be overcome.

The sense of touch also comes into play when tack and equipment is being fitted and used. An ill-fitting saddle which causes not just pressure or friction, but actual pain, produces no end of problems when the horse is ridden, the most common of which are bucking and an apparent refusal to 'go forward'. Ill-fitting bridles cause head-tossing and shaking, resistance to the bit (if it is too high) or getting the tongue over the bit (if it is too low), and general non-acceptance of the bit if the noseband is fastened too tightly.

# CONFORMATION AND ACTION

The skill of purpose-breeding horses is something man has worked at for thousands of years and it is now a refined art. From the few basic types of horse and pony available when the horse first started to be domesticated around 6,000 years ago, we now have hundreds of breeds and types worldwide, some bred for a quality as insignificant as colour but most for specific working attributes such as jumping ability, speed, exaggerated gaits, agility, calm temperament, strength and so on. So we get everything from tiny miniature ponies to massive draught horses, but by far the majority of horses today come somewhere in between these extremes, in the overall riding horse category that ranges from private hacks to world-class performers in the competition disciplines. Some breeds and families (like the Morgan, which is capable of nearly everything), are bred to multi-task, while others are being developed for, say, both dressage and jumping competitions – but most horses could be more versatile (from our viewpoint) if we let them. Schooling horses for several jobs – cross-training, as it is called now – enriches their lives and makes them more versatile and interesting for us.

If you have, or look for, a horse with good basic conformation for riding you have an excellent chance of taking part in several different disciplines, either for fun or for more serious competition. Although this book cannot cover the subject of conformation and action exhaustively, let's look at a basically well-conformed riding horse and his action to see what to look for in a horse. I'll also consider some common faults which limit what ridden jobs a horse can do.

## Basic Symmetry

In any riding horse, the most important point to look for initially is *symmetry*. Symmetry in form means, in practice, that no one part of the horse should be over-stressed, doing more work than it should, carrying more weight than it should, unbalancing the whole or affecting the horse's easy use of his own body. If he has a fault, it will become much more obvious when he has to carry weight and work that much harder. If he has to work fairly athletically, then any fault will be emphasized much more and, even if he does not strike into himself, he is likely to be using his body unevenly or in a way that takes the weight, force and stress away from the weaker or less-than-perfect part – an adjustment called compensatory movement. Thus a fault in one part of a horse can increase the likelihood of injury occurring not only in that part but also elsewhere as unaccustomed or inappropriate muscles are used to keep going and meet the demands of the work.

Horses' bodies do become stronger in the parts taking on the extra effort but this often leads to uneven muscular development (frequently spotted by trained saddle fitters, vets, physical therapists and good teachers and trainers). This, in turn, can lead to problems under saddle which can give you, the rider, the idea that the horse is being difficult and may cause you to ride in a – shall we say – stronger way than you would normally if you do not understand what is really happening or how to put it right.

Before starting to assess a horse, remember that no horse is perfect – although a few are nearly so. Imperfection does not mean that an animal with a noticeable fault cannot do any job at all. It is often a matter of the degree of the fault and what you want to do with the horse. The better you understand your own horse's conformation and action, the easier it will be for you to understand what problems your horse has as a consequence and what you can do to help him. His basic conformation is determined by the form of his skeleton and you cannot change that but you can, provided his faults are not too marked, give him particular schooling exercises to develop his muscles in a way which will help him counteract them.

Try to study as many horses and ponies as you can with an inquiring eye and look for proportion, a horse who 'fills your eye' and in whom your eye is not drawn to one part more than others: if that is the case, that will almost certainly be the part of the body which either has a definite fault or which does not fit in with the balance of the whole.

One example of this is the apparent shape of the horse's neck. Because many horses today are ridden in a way which 'squashes' in the neck, this can give the impression of the horse being out of proportion. A good way to get your eye in is to look at in-hand showing classes (those in which horses are stood up and allowed to move naturally, not those in which it is common practice to stand horses up with their heads held high and their hind legs stretched out, or in side-reins) and study those whom the judges place at the top end of the line. Also, watch horses at liberty moving around with their friends or being worked loose. Look at photos of similar subjects in magazine articles and show reports and buy or borrow books, DVDs and videos on conformation and action. Once you're getting a reliable idea of what a winner looks like, you can start studying horses at the bottom end of an in-hand showing class line-up or looking for faults in the horses you see in fields and paddocks.

So, now, let's get precise. Get out your camera and start snapping any horses or ponies anywhere who are standing naturally, head up and on all fours, ideally looking straight ahead into the distance. Take photos square-on from the side with your camera absolutely level and the lens pointing at a spot two-thirds of the way down the ribcage, in a straight line down from the withers. Do not tilt the camera to point at this spot: keep it horizontal and bend your knees or stand on tiptoe, as necessary. This is because any tilting of the camera, or taking the photo with the horse angled towards or away from the lens, or tilting the camera to left or right, will produce a distorted picture of the horse. Get prints or print-outs of these photos, a ruler and a pen, and assess the horses according to the following basic blueprint.

Before you say that all horses are different and they cannot all fit into a one-size-fits-all plan, I'd point out that, actually, decently made horses do, more or less. The *three main points* you need to look for and measure to assess basic symmetry are:

1. Measuring horizontally, the distance from the poll to the point of the withers and from the withers to the croup should be the same or very nearly so, and the distance from the croup to the root of the tail should be roughly half the latter.
2. Measuring vertically, the distance from the withers to the girth/breastbone should be at least half the distance from the withers to the ground, and the distance from the croup to the ground should be the same as the latter, or very nearly so.
3. Measuring down the side of the horse's head, the length of the head should be very nearly the same as the length of the neck.

## Specific Points
### THE HEAD AND NECK

The horse's head and neck are equivalent to our arms insofar as they act like a balancing pole. The horse cannot move effectively without fairly free use of them; indeed completely free use of them when jumping. Unfortunately, the trend in riding in many quarters today is to hold the head and neck firmly in place, which forces the horse to use compensatory movement with the risk of injury to other parts of his body. As mentioned earlier, many ridden horses actually look as though they have short necks in proportion to the rest of the body whereas, when the same horses are able to use a freer head and neck carriage, it can be seen that they are, in fact, quite normally conformed, and move better.

A long neck, especially with a large head on the end of it, can make it hard for the horse to balance and move well since such features pull him on to his forehand. A long neck with a smallish head is not so bad in this respect, a remark that also applies to a combination of a short neck and a large head. However, a naturally high carriage of head and neck (that is, as a consequence of skeletal structure) is not good as this often means that the horse goes with a hollow back and that it is difficult for his hind legs and quarters to engage under him for carrying power and thrust. Also, he will be difficult to persuade to flex to the bit as he is naturally 'above the bit'.

The throat should be arched, not angular, and open enough to fit a man's fist between the round jawbones, to allow for an unimpeded windpipe and clear airflow (provided his head-carriage is not overly restricted).

## THE TRUNK

For good general balance, the withers and croup should be the same height. Croup-high horses (with the croup higher than the withers) give the sensation of riding downhill and create saddle-fitting problems with pressure behind the shoulders and elbows. Many sprint-bred racehorses and jumpers are a little croup-high as, combined with well-muscled hindquarters and strong hind legs, this conformation provides a lot of power for explosive speed and thrust over fences. Such horses, though, may have difficulty in 'sitting' on to their hindquarters for collected movements. Withers-high horses are 'built uphill' and generally sought-after for dressage for the 'feel' they give and the impression of being able to lower their quarters into collection (and often the natural ability to do so).

The line of the shoulder-blade rising from the point of the shoulder to the withers should generally be at an angle of very nearly 45 degrees to the ground, with the foot-pastern axis (the line up the front of the foot and pastern seen from the side) matching this. These angles give good absorption of shock forces up the foreleg (the hind pasterns are usually slightly more upright, which gives more practical strength for pushing the horse forwards). A horse of the proportions detailed, with this angulation of the shoulder (known as a 'well laid-back' shoulder) gives the rider the secure feeling of having 'plenty in front' of the saddle. Looked at from the side, the point of the elbow should come in front of a line dropped vertically from the highest point of the withers, and you should be able to fit the width of three fingers between the inside of the elbow and the horse's ribcage for an open elbow, which allows for free foreleg reach.

The breastbone should run parallel to the ground for its length, followed by a belly rising gently up towards the stifles. Sagging bellies, though, are often found in older horses who have lost muscular tone, broodmares, horses who have never been schooled to go properly (with their backs and bellies up) and those who are overweight. Ideally, there should be a natural girth groove in the girth area a little behind the shoulders/elbows: such a horse, with moderately high withers, is conformed to be able to 'carry a saddle' securely without it slipping sideways, forwards or backwards – a real boon in a riding horse.

The measurements from withers to breastbone (girth) and from breastbone to ground are important in giving the horse lung room for a good airflow during active work (known misleadingly as 'heart room', and being 'deep in the girth') and to ensure that he is not too long in the leg ('showing too much daylight') for agility and good balance.

The trunk should be roomy but comfortable to sit on. Normally, an oval-shaped ribcage in the girth area, swelling out behind the rider's leg, indicates comfort and substance. A too-narrow horse ('slab-sided') gives an insecure feeling and restricted lung room, whereas one too wide and round in the ribcage can be uncomfortable and difficult to get your legs round, and will give an unpleasant, rolling way of going.

The measurement from croup to root of tail tells whether or not the hindquarters are long enough to allow for plenty of muscle and for its potential development. Short quarters do not usually have the power for speed or thrust, specifically for jumping and sprinting.

A good horse's back will dip slightly behind the withers, run straight and then rise gently over wide, muscular loins and up to the croup, dipping slightly to the root of the tail, the whole giving a smoothly undulating appearance. An arched (roached) back or a dipped (sway) one are both faults which significantly affect comfort and performance. You should just be able to fit the width of your hand between the last rib and the point of the hip: such a horse is called 'well ribbed up'. A very short space here makes for strength but occasionally a slight lack of flexibility, and such horses often overreach. Conversely, a larger space means that the horse is 'slack in the loins' and may have a slightly weak back and lack of agility.

The tail should be set on about level with the horse's back and be carried loosely and swinging, arched according to the horse's breed and type.

# THE LIMBS AND THEIR ATTACHMENT

Take some photos of your equine models from square-on in front, with the camera lens pointing horizontally straight at the chest, and then from behind with the lens aiming at the point where the thigh muscles curve away towards the thighs. Get someone to hold the tail to the side so you get a clear view.

What you are looking for, conformation-wise, is a horse who has 'a leg at each corner' – in other words, he can stand four-square on his hooves when he wants to or when you ask him to, without his feet or limbs being off line or turning in or out (although see later for a little-understood point about the hind legs).

Clearly, without four sound legs and feet a horse is no good for work, and his ability to remain sound depends a great deal on the conformation of his limbs. The forelegs, in particular, bear a lot of stress and strain from the weight and forces put on them by the propulsive force of the hindquarters, their own weight, that of the rider and saddle, the speed at which the horse is asked to travel and the height and width of any obstacles he is asked to negotiate. It is often said that 'speed is the killer' but so is the size of jumps.

Most horses, even those with quite noticeably suspect legs and feet, can be used for gentle hacking, but if they are wanted for anything more involving marked physical effort – work as opposed to just exercise, longish rides, speed, agility and jumping – good, sound limbs and feet are highly desirable if we want them to remain sound enough for work most of the time. Some injuries to athletically working horses are pretty much inevitable, but good conformation combined with sound judgement, due care, good management and farriery go a long way towards keeping any horse sound. Starting off with badly made limbs is giving both you and the horse a handicap from the beginning, as he is much more likely to suffer stresses and strains than a well-made horse. (It has to be said, though, that some really peculiarly shaped horses, and some with actual deformities, have worked remarkably satisfactorily for years, even at high levels).

A fact often overlooked is that the legs begin at the shoulders and hips, not the elbows and stifles. Unlike humans, horses have no collar-bone and no bony joint linking the shoulders to the ribcage. The chest and front part of the ribcage are supported in a structure of muscles, tendons, ligaments and other soft tissues known as the 'thoracic sling'. This is a good arrangement for a horizontally structured running animal as it absorbs impact coming up the forelegs from the ground and forward along the spine from the hindquarters without jarring the shoulder joints. It also avoids the 'crocodilian' stance, with the body sagging between widely spaced limbs, which doesn't make for fluidity of movement.

The hindquarters, conversely, do have a joint linking the pelvis to the hind limbs – the hip joint. This is not the 'point of the hip' (actually the wing of the pelvis) but lower and further back and in – just forward from and level with the point of the buttock inside the hindquarters.

The lumbo-sacral joint at the croup is a crucial joint for obtaining tilting or engagement of the pelvis/hindquarters and, because of the link via the hip joints, the engagement of the hind legs, too. This engagement is necessary for the horse to develop good thrust and carrying/lifting power with his hind legs 'under him' rather than trailing out behind, where they are much less effective. You can see this engagement not only in properly schooled riding horses but also in jumpers and racehorses at the gallop. Horses with moderately rounded hindquarters and well-marked, open stifles should be able to engage without too much trouble (if taught correctly) but those with flat croups and hindquarters often find it difficult to engage the hindquarters/pelvis and to bring their hind legs more forward underneath them. They often trail their hind legs and can tend towards back problems because they do not go in the 'vertebral bow' posture, in which the horse holds himself with his spine lifted slightly, for strength and stability (see also Chapter 9).

## THE FORELIMBS

Looked at from in front, you should be able to draw a line on your photo(s) dropping straight down from the point of the shoulder, through the middle of the knee and fetlock and finishing in the centre of the toe. This will mean that weight falls down the limb evenly, without one side of it experiencing more than the other. If the latter occurs, this will be exaggerated under a rider.

Looked at from the side, the forelimbs should fall straight down like columns from elbow to fetlock when the horse is standing four-square, sloping neither forwards nor backwards. The horse should not stand habitually 'leaning' forward over his forefeet, with his forelegs slanting back from elbow to foot, which is a fairly common fault. This makes the horse heavy in hand and difficult to balance and engage, and it stretches and stresses the soft tissues (those essential tendons and ligaments) down the backs of the legs. The reverse stance hollows and stresses the back.

Also from the side, it should be evident that the pasterns should slope at the same angle as the shoulders, a good angle being about 45 degrees, the line down the pastern carrying on down the front of the hoof so that, although there will be a slight bump for the coronet, there is no dipping down at the coronet (known as 'broken back') or rising up (known as 'broken forward').

Horses with upright (less sloping) shoulders and pasterns can give a jarring ride which also means that their forelegs are experiencing this jarring and not absorbing impact very well in the joints of the limbs. This can cause stress injuries. Conversely, horses with very sloping pasterns (which may be rather long, as well) may give a lovely, springy ride, but are putting their tendons and ligaments under more stress than would be the case with a slightly more upright conformation.

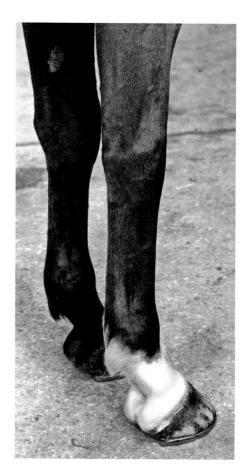

Although the old quote 'No foot, no horse' is very true, we could just as well say 'No legs, no horse'. Any riding horse must have the constitution to remain sound for his job, whatever his type. These legs clearly belong to a 'blood' type horse – a Thoroughbred or a horse very nearly so. The tendons are clear to see and 'clean' with no lumps or bumps and the feet and legs are well conformed. With good care and considerate riding, such a horse should remain sound in suitable work for many years.

## THE HIND LIMBS

Viewed from the side with the horse standing four-square, you should be able to draw a vertical line from the point of the buttock, touching the hock and passing down the back of the cannon bone to the fetlock. The hind pasterns are usually slightly more upright than the fore ones.

If the cannons slope forwards so that the fetlocks are in front of the vertical line, the horse is said to have 'sickle hocks' – a weak structure which predisposes to various hock and soft tissue injuries and unsoundness. If the fetlocks come behind the line (assuming the horse was standing square, for him, when you snapped him) he is said to be 'camped out' or to have his 'hocks in the next county'. This conformation makes it very difficult for him to engage behind and predisposes him to back problems and towards difficulties carrying weight.

Viewed from behind, if the hocks are bowed outwards, often with the feet turning inwards, the weight is not being carried naturally, and the outsides of the legs can experience stretching forces whereas the insides may experience concussive, pressure forces. The reverse conformation, where the hocks incline inwards and the hind feet turn out noticeably is known as 'cow-hocked'. When present to a marked degree, cow hocks present opposite forces on the legs and feet to bowed ones, but still put the legs under uneven stresses and predispose them to injury.

An interesting point to consider is that it is normal for all equines to be *very slightly* cow-hocked and to have the hind feet turning similarly *very slightly* outwards but this tendency, in a working horse, should be so slight that you do have to look for it – it should not 'shout' at you. The opinion has been expressed to me that horses who are bred to have very straight, 'forward-facing' hind legs in this regard can actually experience more hip, hock and hind fetlock stress and unsoundness than others with *slight* cow-hocks.

If you look carefully at a horse from directly in front and behind, you should see that he appears to have only two legs. This means that he is standing four-square and moving straight. His forelegs obscure your view of his hind legs if you are dead in front of him, and his hind legs obscure his forelegs if you are exactly behind him. This is highly desirable conformation and action and, of course, it means that his hind legs and hooves follow exactly the same plane as his forelegs and hooves on straight lines and curves, even if he *is* very slightly cow-hocked and toed out, as described above. This has been a standard gauge of good conformation and what is called 'true' action throughout the ages and with very good reason – such horses are well balanced, normally foot-sure, don't often brush or speedicut and stay sound in significant, reasonable work.

It is often thought that, from a visual assessment, because a horse's hips (points of the hips or, more correctly, the wings of his pelvis) are wider than his shoulders, his hind feet land a little to the outsides of his forefeet, but this is clearly not so in a well-conformed, balanced horse. Seek out a horse with the best conformation and action you can along the above guidelines, ask his rider to walk and trot him on a loose rein without influencing his position in any way (in other words, be a non-interfering rider), and watch him moving along the long sides of an arena, and you will see what I mean.

This has significant implications for us when riding, as it is often taught that you must ride a horse in a manège so that his forehand is brought very slightly in to 'even up' his hoofprints. When you understand that good conformation and action means that the lateral pair of hind and fore prints are on the *same line*, you realize that this is not only unnecessary but undesirable.

As for the width apart of the hooves when the horse is standing square, you should be able to fit another hoof comfortably between both the fore and hind feet. Horses narrow in this respect have a tendency to brush or speedicut (kick themselves on the insides of their legs) and may not be confident in their gaits or as stable in their balance as those with more desirable conformation. They might also be prone to tripping themselves up. Those unusually wide in this regard often give rocking rides and may not be particularly agile.

## THE FEET

Wild and feral horses cannot survive if they do not have four sound, comfortable feet. If the feet are not functional, if they are uncomfortable or hurt, the horse cannot run, cannot escape a predator and will be killed. Domestic horses also need four good, well-made, functional feet if they are to be able to do a job.

Looking at the feet from a conformation viewpoint, balance is just as important as in the body overall.

Seen from underneath, the forefeet are more circular in shape than the hinds, which are more oval. The paired feet should also be the same size, an individual smaller foot often indicating that the horse has had a significant injury or disease in that leg and has been weight-bearing on its opposite pair. This can cause the hoof on the painful leg or foot to become smaller and the weight-bearing one larger.

We have already mentioned the foot-pastern axis (seeing a straight, angled line from the side, up the front of the foot or toe and on up the pastern) but it is worth adding that a foot with a broken-back axis often has low heels and too-long toes, an arrangement that stresses the tendons and ligaments down the back of the leg, and the internal structure of the foot. This foot conformation often indicates laminitis whereas the opposite, a broken-forward axis can indicate navicular disease. The line or angle of the heel should be the same as that of the toe.

Looking at the feet from the front, the two ends of the coronet should be the same height from the ground on each side. The inside wall of the hoof may be very slightly more upright than the outside one.

Variations from normal, good make and shape in the feet can be caused by neglect, particularly whilst the horse has been growing and developing. It is very important that foals' feet receive attention from a good farrier, even just from a monitoring viewpoint, from a few weeks of age. Once the youngster reaches, say, 6–8 months of age and the bones are starting to become less malleable, it is very difficult to make effective corrections to faulty conformation of the feet and legs. Conversely, neglect and failure to correct deviations in youth can condemn a horse from the point of future soundness and working ability.

If faulty conformation of the foot and less-than-true action have been caused by poor farriery in adulthood, gradual improvements can certainly be made by a good farrier.

## The Horse in Action

We have already briefly mentioned true action as seen from in front and behind but we'll look at things in more detail now. It helps to know what kind of action your horse has so that you can ride accordingly and understand what might be going wrong if you are having problems, and how to help your horse. It is surprising how many horses of less-than-brilliant conformation suddenly come to life when in action. Unfortunately, the reverse can also be true. It is often said that if the walk is good or bad, so will the other gaits be, but this does not pan out in practice. Many horses have a 'best gait', and we can work to improve the others, if necessary.

### THE WALK

This is a four-time gait because a full stride has four separate hoof-beats. Since it is a lateral gait (the feet on one side of the horse are placed on the ground, then the feet on the other side), these hoof-beats might be left hind, left fore, right hind, right fore. Walk is a very stable gait because there are usually either two or three feet on the ground and there is no moment of suspension (when the horse is in the air). The only other gait to which this latter point applies is correct rein-back.

In any gait, the main job of the hind limbs is to push the horse onwards, whereas the forelimbs mainly support the weight like the spokes of a wheel. In walk, when the left hind, for example, comes forward, the leg extends, the foot hits the ground and the horse's weight travels over it. The muscles of the hindquarters and upper leg extend the leg backwards while the foot is still on the ground and this is when they push the horse forwards.

## THE TROT

Trot is a two-time gait: two feet in diagonal pairs hit the ground at the same time, two beats making one stride. The horse will move the left hind and right fore together, spring up into the air into the moment of suspension, and land on the right hind/left fore diagonal.

## THE CANTER

This is a called a three-time gait because of the number of hoof-beats heard. However, each sequence of three beats is followed by a moment of suspension, in which no feet are on the ground. As we know, the horse can canter with the right or left fore leading and the footfalls are:

*For right canter* – left hind, right hind and left fore together, then right fore. The horse then bounds up into the moment of suspension and lands with the left hind again, making one full stride.

*For left canter* – right hind, left hind and right fore together, then left fore. Again, the horse has a moment of suspension and lands with the right hind again.

## THE GALLOP

This is like a strung-out canter of four beats. Whereas the other gaits have a clear transition between them the gallop does not but, strictly speaking, the horse is galloping when the gait changes from three beats to four rapid ones. The sequence is:

*For right gallop* – left hind, right hind, left fore and right fore, then the moment of suspension.

*For left gallop* – right hind, left hind, right fore and left fore, then again the moment of suspension.

## THE REIN-BACK

Rein-back is often regarded as being like a backwards walk but, in fact, when performed correctly, its movement is like a backwards trot with no moment of suspension. One diagonal pair of legs moves backwards first then the other, for example left fore and right hind together then right fore and left hind.

## THE JUMP

Even if a horse is not intended for a jumping discipline, teaching horses to jump can be enjoyable for both horse and rider, develops the horse's ability to think (if he is not interfered with), develops strength and agility in the horse and can be a fun way of having a break from other schooling. Gymnastic jumping over small obstacles of varying types and spreads – not to mention grids – is superb mental and physical training for any riding horse.

A horse can jump from a standstill if he needs to, but the easiest gait at which to judge his natural flow and athleticism is canter. If he is going to get his legs all mixed up it is more likely to be when jumping from trot, so trot is a good gait at which to judge his general agility and control.

## Qualities of Gaits

Whatever equestrian discipline(s) you are interested in, a good riding horse has to have certain mechanical qualities in his gaits which humans have desired over the centuries. These have been proven over time to make him a 'good ride', schooling permitting.

We have already mentioned 'true' action – that you should be aware of only two legs when the horse is moving directly towards or away from you. This indicates that the fore and hind limbs are travelling in the same plane, not unduly stressing their structures by uneven weight-bearing caused by moving and landing crookedly, and not wasting energy by moving on a longer 'journey' through the air by swinging inwards or outwards. True action makes the rider's job easier, too, by helping to ensure that the energy forces are directed in a straight and true manner through the horse's body. It is easier to straighten a horse with true action, and achieve impulsion, than one whose action deviates in any way from the desired standard. A straight-moving horse surely finds movement easier than one with crooked action.

As an overall impression, the horse should present a picture of ease, relaxation and swing throughout the body and of covering the ground easily in his gaits. Natural balance and self-control are massive advantages in any riding horse. These are all best judged with the horse at liberty or at least being led on a completely loose rope.

From the side, the horse should be seen to be moving actively and reaching forwards from the shoulders and hips, the shoulder-blades being seen to be mobile and noticeably swivelling around a point about a third of the way down the bone from the withers. An open elbow (remember the three fingers width between the inside of the elbow and the ribcage) will add to the length of reach. If the horse is 'tied in' here his length of stride will be restricted. His feet should land well towards his head when it is held naturally.

In walk, the hind feet should land well in front of the prints of the forefeet, the precise distance depending upon the horse's natural conformation and action. The overtrack (the distance by which they do so) should not be a consequence of a short front or 'tied-in' elbows, both of which shorten the stride in front.

In trot, the foreleg should be arched forwards from a swinging, reaching shoulder so that the horse almost appears to land toe first. (In fact, horses should land with their feet almost flat for good, even absorption of the impact of landing.) The type of action in which the horse flicks his toe up comes from a shallow, flat stride in which the legs are flung out straight rather than arched and reached forward. This flicking type of action stresses and stretches the tendons and ligaments down the backs of the forelegs and is not good. It often indicates that the horse is being urged too fast, is unbalanced, on the forehand and going with his back and belly down instead of raised and with the quarters tilted under so that the hind feet can reach well forwards from a stable base for push and power. Some horses are forced into this action by riders who mistake speed for impulsion, but if they do it naturally it is a disadvantage which can, however, be corrected by schooling.

At the back end, the hind legs must swing forward from the hips and have well-defined stifle action. In working trot, the hind feet should track up, that is, land in the prints of the forefeet. In canter, watch for a free flexion of the croup/lumbo-sacral joint so that the horse naturally tilts his pelvis noticeably and brings his hind feet well forward under his belly. Most horses have a favourite leg with which to lead and may travel slightly quarters-in to that side. Try to get the horse worked loose and watch for this and also for the ease with which he makes his flying changes from one direction or rein to the other as he bounds around the school or paddock. If he raises a gallop, watch how easily he stops, returns to canter, spins round on his hind feet and negotiates his corners. A riding horse needs to be able to move freely and easily at all gaits at liberty: if he does not, your job with him under saddle will be made that much more difficult.

If you can see the horse jump loose, watch for the ease with which he sees his own stride, his attitude to the job in hand, the thrust at take-off, and the fluency with which he flows over the fence, lands and gets away. Any propping stride, stiffness, reluctance, getting 'under' the fences (taking off too close) or jarring on landing will create problems when jumping under saddle. Jumpers also need a moderate degree of joint action in the knees and hocks rather than being 'daisy-cutters' with long, low strides and little use of those joints – the type of action often seen in Thoroughbreds and Arabs and horses with much of their blood. However, not all Thoroughbreds daisy-cut; for instance, most eventers, steeplechasers and point-to-pointers need more joint action here, plus open elbows and stifles, to enable them to easily snap up their legs over their fences.

The issue of short cannons and well let down hocks with long forearms and thighs is important in any riding horse, especially one expected to do athletic work and particularly jumping. The horse should have clearly longer upper legs than lower, with the point of the hock level with the front chestnuts, and the legs should look to be of a proportionate circumference ('amount of bone') for the body type and size of the horse. The forearms and thighs need good muscling, and short cannons are desirable because a short structure is always stronger than a longer one of the same circumference. This conformation makes for strength under the stress of work, and provides good thrust and leverage with less risk of injury than with longer, possibly weaker cannons.

Now let's talk about that delightful quality, cadence, which is bandied about a lot but which is advantageous in any riding horse. A definition of cadence may be that it is the regular, rhythmic sound and feel of a horse's gait, with the horse covering the same amount of ground at each stride (unless asked to lengthen or shorten). Impulsion and elasticity also come into it. Probably the easiest gait in which to assess it is trot. A horse showing cadence often appears to hover in the air *fleetingly* in his moment of suspension. He lands and almost bounces as if on springs with a confident, regular rhythm.

I remember a long time ago there being a discussion in the British equestrian press (but well worthy of *The Times*) as to whether a horse showing cadence spent longer in the air (as had been stated in an article by an eminent horseman) or longer on the ground, and all sorts of learned arguments were put forward on both sides with, as is often the case in the horse world, no consensus of opinion. A physicist joined the fray and said that, unless a horse were using a trampoline, the laws of physics stated that he had to spend equal amounts of time on the ground and in the air. At that point, the editor grasped the opportunity to declare, in time-honoured fashion, that 'this correspondence is now closed'. We never seem to get esoteric arguments like that these days – more's the pity, as they were great fun.

Not all horses have natural cadence and it is exhilarating to ride and to see, particularly in horses at liberty. It can be improved with schooling and subtle riding, when the horse has learnt to balance under his rider and go confidently from his hindquarters.

Finally, I must mention the fashionable aim of athleticism in gaits. 'Athletic' gaits seem to be the first box on the tick-list these days in some disciplines, yet the gaits presented often are not indicative of actual athleticism but are merely over-exaggerated and strained, particularly in extended trot, and look either ridiculous or upsetting depending on your viewpoint. On the other hand, elastic, elegant and *naturally* extravagant gaits presented with skill, and care for the horse, are a dream to watch and sit on. Particularly in the competition horse field, breeding for action is a predictable art. A really athletic mover is impressive to watch, either in the field or during work, but most horse's gaits can be enhanced by fitness, good farriery, physical therapy and appropriate muscular development through correct schooling and training. Let's just be sure that, in our desire to impress, we do not produce farcical versions of what the horse already has to give.

We cannot leave this topic without mention of what has, for hundreds of years, been regarded as the correct head-carriage. Read any of the most respected books on equitation and you will see the correct head carriage to aim for in a schooled, made horse described as having the poll as the highest point and the front line of the face, seen from the side, as being just in front of an imaginary, vertical line dropped from his forehead to the ground. Some texts say that the horse may be just 'on the vertical', and this may be so if his head is naturally set on to his neck in such a way as to make this appropriate for him. This is the case in many Iberian horses (those originating in Spain and Portugal), for instance, but this is different in many Thoroughbred and Arab horses and their crosses, who have a head-carriage in which the nose is naturally a good deal in front of a vertical line.

In some disciplines, we often see horses presented with their faces behind the vertical – which has *never* been regarded as good or correct by the best authors, trainers and riders. This is partly because no horse goes naturally at liberty with his head in that position for more than a few seconds (as when tossing his head and playing) and partly because, owing to the way the horse's eyes are set in his skull and the way they function, unless he looks upward all the time he cannot see properly straight ahead when the head is in this position – which is unkind to say the least, and potentially dangerous, especially when jumping or travelling over tricky ground. There is also evidence that compelling a horse to go in this posture injures the bone and soft tissues of the poll and neck and probably causes pain and tension in the muscles of the neck and shoulders. Faced with the consequential discomfort, the horse will use the rest of his body in compensatory ways to avoid it and the whole presents a sorry picture to the knowledgeable and caring observer.

There is an argument that some horses carry their heads naturally in this position and so it is not a fault but, as mentioned above, no horse goes naturally in this position for more than a very few seconds at liberty. *It is the way a horse goes naturally, at liberty, that we need to use as our benchmark for judging action.* If a ridden horse appears to be going in this way voluntarily, even on a light, long or loose/free rein, it is most likely to be because he is trying to avoid the feel or action of the bit in his mouth, or is *expecting* discomfort on that score. This is known as being 'behind the bit' and has long been acknowledged as a fault. (In fact, it is a fault of a rider, past or present, not the horse.) It could also be because the horse has been made or 'schooled' to go in this way and now does so out of habit. Either way, the argument does not hold water.

All the above points and qualities of conformation and action state the ideal and there is no such thing as an absolutely perfect horse in this respect – they say. Horses are living, breathing flesh and blood, and very many good horses are, as they also say, 'very hard to fault'. I have seen many horses I regard as perfect, but then I am not a perfectionist. Horses, like people and other animals, are individuals and all different. With a good understanding of conformation and action, plus the ability to recognize those indefinable and intangible qualities of presence, spirit and individuality, you may well come to realize that there are more 'perfect' horses, to you, than you ever dreamed of.

## THE JOB FOR THE HORSE

There is a multitude of breeds and types of horse and pony and many are multi-talented. Good *all-rounders* make ideal family horses and mounts for keen amateur riders and for these you need the good, basic classical conformation described above. Horses with that sort of conformation and action but with variations in that hard-to-describe quality of 'type' can make hacks, hunters and riding horses and, provided they have the inclination, can turn their hooves to almost anything. For showing you also need that famous 'look at me' quality called 'presence', plus an energetic but calm temperament and straight, eye-catching action.

*Horses intended for dressage* are specifically bred with 'uphill' conformation and carriage these days but, of course, any well-made, straight- and free-actioned horse would fill the bill, depending on the level at which you want to compete. Naturally extravagant but true action is a definite asset. Many riders like dressage horses to be slightly long in the back, which is felt to make 'bend' easier to achieve, and clearer to the judge. (I'm putting bend in quotation marks because, as explained in The Skeleton and Spinal Movement in Chapter 9, the degree to which the horse can truly 'bend' laterally is very limited.) A good, naturally rounded top-line is desired, with no tendency towards a 'plank' neck, a thick or angular jowl or an inclination to find it hard to flex. Although many people's attention is easily centred on the forehand, neck and head, it is the hindquarters that need particular attention, as these provide the thrust and carrying power for the various gaits and movements: for that, you need very well-made and correct quarters, and hind legs with strong musculature. At present, big horses are sought for dressage as it is felt that they are more impressive, but this must not be at the expense of balance and agility indeed, it is ironic, really, since given the same relative proportions, temperament, etc., a smaller horse is more manoeuvrable and gives the rider a fraction more operating time.

For *jumping*, you need a well-balanced horse who is definitely not inclined to hot up. All the talent in the world is useless if you can't control it, so a calm, amenable temperament is essential – and a bit of natural nous is also a great help. For the power and thrust required, you need particularly good hindquarters with long, well-muscled thighs from stifle to hock and also a long forearm and large, flat knee. Balance is crucial in jumpers, so a moderately long neck with a proportionate head is needed – plus a rider who allows the horse to use them. At the higher levels, a bit of height is an asset in a jumper, so long as this does not make the horse ungainly and clumsy.

For any kind of *speed* work, whether it is jumping against the clock or bursts of energy such as in polo, you need overall naturally well-developed musculature – a compact horse with strength, balance and agility. Keenness and determination are assets of temperament which fuel the horse during demanding but relatively short stints of work.

Work involving *stamina* such as cross-country, hunting in a galloping country and endurance work usually suits lean, sometimes even rather raw-boned horses, with long rather than chunky muscles and a lot of lung room. A ground-eating stride is a massive help in sports like this. Again, a controllable, calm temperament is particularly helpful in a horse who needs to conserve his energy and maybe work for long periods; a 'hyper' type who frets away nervous energy early on in the proceedings may 'run out of petrol' at the crucial moment. Smaller horses are usually preferred for endurance riding, as it is generally felt by competitors that they are handier, more agile, and that their gaits and metabolisms work more efficiently than those of larger horses, thereby offering greater stamina – but reasonable height is generally an advantage in other disciplines.

## WORKING WITH THE HORSE'S MIND

Great strides have been made in the sciences of equine behaviour and psychology in recent decades and the techniques which have long been proven, effective and standard practices in the training of other species are being applied to horses in ways appropriate to their mental functioning. As explained earlier, horses, in many ways, certainly do not think like humans and the way their senses work gives them a rather different perception of the world from ours, producing behaviour which many people misunderstand and therefore react to inappropriately.

People may be tired of reading and hearing that horses are classic prey animals and are made for life in the great outdoors, but these are facts which govern their mentality and outlook on life, and we can't get away from them. The overriding trait horses possess is a hard-wired tendency to run first when they perceive or suspect danger and stop to look and think later, when they feel far enough away from the danger or are aware that it isn't near them any more. While, instinctively, they cannot help but do this, the tendency can be greatly damped down with training, good experiences, trust and consequential modifications of habit. For example, this innate tendency is why some horses are so ready to spook and shy, but while such behaviour can quickly become a habit, it is also one which can be 'overlaid' or trained out of them.

Herd life is a safer existence for an animal like a horse because there is relative safety in numbers. A single horse is completely vulnerable to a predator, whereas only one will be required from a group to feed the family of a wild feline or canine species. Also, of course, many eyes and ears provide greater early warning than single pairs. This is why the massive majority of horses only feel secure when in company. Although some appear to tolerate solitude, very, very few prefer a solitary life.

Being naturally herd animals, young horses have to be taught gradually to work alone and those who won't leave the stable yard or who nap and jib when working alone (either in an arena or out hacking) are more likely to be feeling afraid and insecure than trying to get out of work – although the latter *may* happen. At the root of napping from insecurity lies the fact that the horse does not regard his rider as sufficiently trustworthy to replace other horses. It's a relationship issue. But napping in specific locations can become a habit because the horse has associated a particular place or situation with this reaction. However, like shying and spooking, it, too, can be remedied.

Acute perception of the tiniest nuances of the body language of other horses and other species, and of minor changes in the appearance of their surroundings, is another trait naturally possessed by the horse. Anything different, particularly to inexperienced horses (of any age), can mean 'danger'. Wild or feral equines need to be able to read the intentions of a predatory animal (is it hunting or just passing?) and this acute observational skill is what has kept the species going for so long. Horses are also highly accomplished at forming mind maps or remembering places they have been to before – whether it was where water can be found in the wild and where they were once hunted by predators, or where they went on a hack, or to a competition. Domesticated horses use these abilities all the time and therefore when handling, training or schooling and riding, we have to be very consistent in what we do, what aids and signals we give and even how we look and smell. Of course, horses can take in changes, but we have to understand that they first need to assess them and decide whether they bring safety or danger with them.

It is clear that horses used to changing homes, including moving from one livery yard to another in the same ownership, become very experienced at weighing up new places. They do, in my experience and opinion, know somehow whether the place is temporary or permanent and many horses will settle quickly if they sense that the atmosphere is good from their point of view – that there are other, happy horses around, that they have food, water, shelter, a comfortable bed, safe and appealing grazing and competent people caring for them. The reverse is also true, of course. Most horses, because of their natural ability, can weigh up people, places and other horses very quickly indeed.

Horses who are unused to changing home can go through quite a troubling and confusing time when they do so and all the smells, sights, sounds, people and animals and the new people's ways of doing things are different. Different vocal commands and physical aids can be quite worrying for some horses and, when buying a horse, it is always a good idea to ask a previous owner exactly what words and aids were used and how they were applied, in the same way that you would ask about his diet and management. If someone else is going to ride your horse, it will help if you tell them the words you use and perhaps how you apply your aids. The horse will surely get used to different riders if you make this part of his life but, particularly with an inexperienced horse, he may take a little while to take in different techniques.

Having said that, general adaptability is a well-known trait of horses. They *do* adapt to new people, homes, friends, jobs and environments – they assess the changes, and, though the timescale may vary, adapt to them and 'settle in' – because it is a basic survival technique for us all, to adapt or perish. Horses are generally much better at it than some humans!

## The Horse's Capacity for Learning

Horses learn both good and bad things (from our viewpoint) very quickly and seem to remember at least as well as elephants! They learn from every situation or occurrence in their lives (not only when we think we are formally training them), so we have to be certain that we teach them clearly what we want them to know and try to avoid bad associations. This is an awesome responsibility.

There seems to be much more learning capacity in a horse's head than we previously believed – provided we teach everything clearly, consistently and in a way the horse understands. Some people claim that horses are not very intelligent because they have small brains compared with the size of their bodies, but horses actually seem to be very intelligent when it comes to surviving in the environment in which they evolved. The mental and physical features of any species evolve according to what fits it for its natural enviroment, so the horse as a species has everything it needs, both mentally and physically, to survive brilliantly in a grassy plains environment.

Also, let us not forget their adaptability, which enables them to accustom themselves quite well to different circumstances, such as those they encounter in domesticated situations. Being ridden is completely alien to them in nature; indeed, a predatory animal on a horse's back can mean death and the way in which horses are 'thrown in the deep end' to make them rideable in some cultures must be terrifying. It is far better and more rewarding, to those who care about them and do not just pay lip service to it, to accustom a horse gradually to all the procedures and paraphernalia of being backed, ridden and schooled, taking advantage of his traits for adaptability and learning quickly.

Horses soon learn what commands and aids mean if they are taught in a calm way and by a logical, structured system, using instant reward following a correct (desired) response, so that responding as we wish becomes a habit. Calmness is an essential prerequisite to learning because a horse who is not calm (being either excited, upset or frightened) does not develop good associations and cannot learn: all he can do is follow his instinct for self-preservation and try to get out of the situation. This means to him 'flee or fight', and he cannot learn anything we regard as good when he has this mindset.

Techniques and methods commonly used in training horses which make them excited, upset or frightened are:

- Causing discomfort or pain, either from misuse of whip, spurs or bit, badly-fitting tack and equipment, or from strapping the horse up with gadgets or using techniques which force his body into a particular shape or posture and cause aches and pains.

- Shouting.
- Confusing the horse with unclear or conflicting commands or aids (usually a case of bad timing or lack of technical skill on the part of the rider or trainer).
- Asking the horse to do something of which he is incapable, or for which he is not ready.
- Working him in an unpleasant environment such as a dusty school, extremes of weather, or difficult or unsafe going such as a deep or rough school surface.
- Drilling the horse with infrequent rests, or working for too long a session.
- Working the horse whilst unwell or unsound.
- Working without shoes when the horse needs them.
- Generally harsh, unsympathetic riding.

## Reasoning Power

It has long been held by many experienced horse people and the scientifically trained that horses have no reasoning power. This is because they do not have an enlarged right neocortex and prefrontal cortex – the parts of the brain responsible for higher mental functions like reasoning, which are present only in humans, great apes, dolphins and whales. (In this regard, it is worth considering whether or not these functions in the horse are performed by a different part of the brain, as can be the case in some brain-damaged people in whom a different part of the brain takes over functions lost owing to injury or disease.)

Other people, including some vets and equine and animal scientists, disagree and claim to have had experiences or run experiments proving reasoning ability (I come into that category). Yet others argue that horses may have learned to respond 'correctly' by initially doing so accidentally and have associated the act with some instant reward such as food, the cessation of an aid or getting free from the stable, then, having made the association/link, developed the habit of acting/responding in that way. This is quite feasible, of course, but does not seem, to me, to account for the situations in which the horse has clearly had to think about what to do, for instance, a horse who jumps out of fields to get to another field or somewhere else he wants to be.

## Concentration

Although, as mentioned earlier, horses probably have a greater capacity for learning than used to be thought, there are limits to how much they can be expected to absorb in a given period and they should not be trained intensively for more than a very few minutes at a time (about 5, in my experience) without a break, whether that involves just standing still with no demands or walking around on a loose rein or rope to relax. We all know that many horses are schooled for much longer than this in one session without even being given a break on a long rein. This is not horse-friendly because it bullies horses into submitting and it is counter-productive because horses 'switch off', become unhappy and start experiencing physical discomfort and pain, which causes muscles to be sore long after the session has ended.

Intensive mental concentration can only be sustained by humans for about 25 minutes, so it is quite unreasonable to expect horses to achieve anything like that length of time. Within a schooling session of, say, 40 minutes, including warm-up time, it is fair to expect a horse to work and concentrate for about 5 minutes, then have a short break of a minute or two walking around in a relaxed way on a loose, not merely long, rein and being allowed to stretch and look around. Then he can start work again refreshed mentally and rested physically. This sort of regime varies from horse to horse, but I find that horses are much more settled in their work and actually want to take part once they realize that they are never browbeaten or made very tired or uncomfortable during their lessons.

So, taking into account the following factors:

- The horse's propensity for instinctively wanting to get away from anything frightening or distressing.
- The need for fairly instant reward to occur after an act or aid in order for the horse to form an association between them.
- The confusing nature of badly timed and unclear aids.
- The horse's limited capacity, time-wise, for effective learning.

We can say that we understand the basics of riding and schooling horses in a horse-friendly way.

# BODY LANGUAGE AND BEHAVIOUR

Horses communicate their feelings to us mainly by means of their physical attitudes and expressions, and by their behaviour. Some gifted people certainly seem able to communicate with them on a mind-to-mind basis but, whilst this could be really enlightening, it is not practical for most people on an everyday basis. What is needed is a fair understanding of equine body language. The better you understand the 'nuts and bolts' of how your horse looks and what he is doing, the better you will be able to understand what is going on inside his head and the more sensitive you should become to his feelings. It should reach the point, with a normally sensitive person, where you just know how he is at any particular time. Just a glance or a feel is enough and, remember, horses do this with us and other animals already – this is their way of understanding.

Just as importantly, you will be able to tell at once how other people's horses are feeling and what emotions they are betraying with their body language. This will enable you to judge just how well these horses are really being ridden – whether it is horse-friendly or not – and you could be in for quite a few surprises which may alter your estimation of those riders one way or the other.

## *A Physical Language*

It has to be admitted that a large part of understanding equine body language involves being able to spot and 'feel' general tension and unease, but this ability will come with practice if you leave your mind open to the horse and do not make assumptions. Re-read the information given in the Introduction on who and what to ignore whilst assessing a horse and follow your intuition, which will develop the more you use it with an open mind, not 'telling it what you think', for instance.

*Take an overall view* and see if the horse seems tense or worried. The head and face are very expressive in horses and give you at least three-quarters of the information you want.

Horses tend to raise their heads a little when they feel tense or anxious and the skin seems to tighten on their faces, their necks stiffen and their muzzles become tight and mobile or distorted. If they are actually frightened, perhaps experiencing or expecting pain, they will try to get their heads well up out of harm's way unless they are prevented from doing so and the entire body will be stiff and defensive, as if trying to run away.

In times of tension, anxiety or fear, the eyes may be wide and may show the whites, and the ears will be directed towards whatever is bothering them. They may move more stiffly than usual and the tail may be held arched if the horse is excited or upset, clamped down if the horse is frightened, or swishing and thrashing about if he is angry or irritated.

A horse experiencing problems in his mouth, whether from dental pain, other injury, inappropriate bitting arrangements/use of the bit, or too tight a noseband will show this in his muzzle (too mobile, nostrils flaring or wrinkled up and back) and may champ the bit noticeably instead of mouthing it gently. A real giveaway of mouth problems is that horses froth far too much and even drool saliva, maybe even splashing their chests and forearms. *While a moderate degree of lubrication is desirable, it is absolutely not the case that the more froth there is, the better. Although it is now widely believed that it is a sign of a horse happy and comfortable, and with a soft mouth, this is not true: excessive salivation and frothing are signs of distress in mammals.*

Domineering riding or posture enforced by incorrectly (usually too tightly) adjusted training equipment also produces horses who are distressed in one way or another. Often, particularly in an angry horse, the ears will be pressed hard back and down against the neck, the nostrils, again, will be wrinkled up and back and there will be an angry look in the eye with a tense expression on his face. If the horse is helplessly accepting this treatment, his eyes may appear sunken and dull and his performance will lack natural sparkle and joy.

Horses who are upset or frightened often sweat unreasonably for the amount or type of work they are doing. They may 'play up' or, on the other hand, perform like zombies because they have learnt that there is no way out. Much depends on their temperament.

Let's compare all this with the appearance and 'feel' of a willing, happy horse, enjoying his work and his partnership with his rider.

The ears may be pricked forward towards, for instance, an obstacle if he is jumping, or directed softly back towards the rider. They may flick independently towards something catching the horse's attention and back towards the rider. The horse's eyes will be bright and interested, with a soft look or an animated light, depending on the nature of his work.

His muzzle will be held normally and neither it nor his face will appear tight or tense. The nostrils will be functioning normally, too, flaring and narrowing as he breathes. His mouth will be moist and there will be little noticeable froth. He may well be playing *gently* with the bit (which is desirable), allowed to do so by a rider with a sensitive contact and by a noseband that is *not* tight.

The body and the gaits will have an athletic, loose swing and spring to them which will be quite noticeable and, from behind, the back will be seen to swing up and down and the ribcage from side to side as the horse moves: the tail will move with the back *from the dock*, swinging from side to side. (Look carefully to see if it is just the hair that is swinging rather than the dock.) This applies even in a gaily arched tail. A stiff tail (and back) indicate tension, fear, pain or great difficulty in performing.

The horse will not appear contorted in his posture or show exaggerated action in any way. His neck, not being held in by a hard contact, will not appear shortened and out of proportion to the rest of his body. If he is a green or young horse, his neck will be naturally held out and may be down, depending on what his rider is working on, and, if he is being asked to accept the bit, he will be doing so without signs of distress or dislike. A more advanced horse will also not look tense in the neck but will be holding it in an arched shape which is clearly being stretched forward and up, with the front of his face in front of a vertical line dropped from his poll to the ground, and with his poll the highest point of his outline (apart from his ears). His gaits will be elastic, joyful and natural and the whole picture pleasant to watch.

Such a horse is being ridden in a horse-friendly way, for certain.

It is also good to assess the rider (no matter who he or she is, what reputation or qualifications they have or what they have won). A correctly held seat, depending on the discipline, will clearly come from fitness and use. Stiffness plays no part in the position of a good rider. A rider who is clearly ramrod stiff, even though technically 'correct', is not helping or 'supporting' the horse at all but indicating that the two of them are not a 'pair'. This is enough to spoil the gaits and attitude of most horses.

Look at the rider's hands and arms and see if you can sense any give and take in them, or whether they are holding the horse's head and neck in a vice-like grip – in which case the horse will clearly show it in his posture and facial expression. Do you detect harsh use of the bit, jabbing at the mouth, a fixed, rigid hand or, horror of horrors, sawing at the bit? Do you notice abusive use of spurs or whip and is the rider's facial expression so hard you could 'strike a match on it' (the graphic expression of a friend of mine)?

A horse-friendly rider will be quietly confident, still but clearly in good control of his or her seat and position. There will be ample give and take on the reins, as appropriate, and the hands will generally be 'there', gentle and still, and held in a straight line between the elbow and the horse's mouth. The seat and small of the back will be seen to be mobile, absorbing the movements of the horse's back. The upper body and head, generally, will be still.

There will be no harsh use of bit, spurs or whip and the rider will not fidget around in the saddle, out of balance and with legs and hands flying around. Riders often develop their own individual styles and, even at the highest levels, we can see the most amazing acrobatics performed habitually by some riders. I maintain that they would do even better if they rode better and kept stiller, so that they did not upset their horses' balance or diverted their attention with movements which the horses had to decipher as being aids or not. This is too much of a burdensome responsibility for an animal who has enough to think about as it is.

A skilled, caring and competent true horseman or horsewoman is, like a horse being ridden well, a joy and a thrill to watch. With a bit of practice, you will be able to pick out both and probably find both instructive, revealing and entertaining.

# CHAPTER 2

# At What Age Should You Start?

Horses are normally regarded as mature at 6 or 7 years of age and, to gauge lifespan, we can say that one year to us is about three and a half or four years to a horse. Feral horses live to very roughly 12 years of age but domesticated ones now regularly live and often work well into their twenties. A horse is still said to be 'aged' at 8 years but this does not mean aged as in old, it means well matured and in his prime, which has commonly extended, for general reckoning, between the ages of 8 and 12. A horse was, until very recently, said to be old at 15 and some insurance companies still use this cut-off point for insurance purposes, insuring after this age for accidents but not illnesses.

However, with improved nutrition, veterinary care and correct, fair working, our horses are living active lives much longer than ever before. Of course, the emphasis must always be on a sound, all-round regime of care and good management, which gives the horse every chance to work well and also to be content with his life. Any horse can be broken down and finished early if he is worked too hard for his levels of development and fitness; if he is managed and worked incorrectly (which places unreasonable stresses and strains on his body and mind); if he is not fed well and correctly with regard to an appropriate balance of nutrients (not only vitamins and minerals); is not given good veterinary care or is worked in a job for which he is just not best suited.

Although horses on average seem to be working well and living longer than in earlier times, unfortunately, at the other end of their lives, things are not always so rosy – particularly for those from talented parents. There is still an element which regards them as disposable and dispensable. The world of equestrian competition expands and, along with some sublime riding, there are also some appalling displays at all levels of most disciplines which, disgracefully, are not always penalized. As in the sport of racing in the nineteenth and twentieth centuries, money becomes a bigger and bigger factor and people want quicker returns on their investments. This often places unreasonable pressures on the very horses without whom the sports would not be possible. They are bred and fed to develop early and are often brought into significant work much too early in their lives.

Although, to some extent, the body develops and adapts in accordance with the stresses placed upon it, there are limits. Newly weaned foals should not be jumping metre-high fences which, apparently, is expected of them in some quarters. (I give further on in this chapter a slightly flexible curriculum of what horses can reasonably and fairly be expected to do at various ages.) Training and work always place demands on their minds as well as their bodies (and let's not forget their spirits) and all individuals vary, but the timescale given, maybe with minor differences, has been proven over the years, by caring and knowledgeable handlers and trainers, to be fair and reasonable if carried out skilfully.

Discipline must certainly be instilled, as it is in a herd of other horses, but discipline does not comprise either overt or covert brutality involving physical pain or frightening and confusing mind games. I am firmly of the view that horses need boundaries. I do not agree with the principle of praising a horse for 'doing well' but ignoring misdemeanours or mistakes. In a herd, horses are left in no doubt about what is acceptable and what is not acceptable to, first, their dams and, as time goes on, their herd mates.

We humans have the added advantage of being able to use our voices to praise and correct in an appropriate tone, using consistent words for commands and letting the horse know how we feel – a short, sharp 'No' in a cross tone but without shouting if the horse is definitely being 'naughty', or expressed more gently if he simply needs telling or reminding that something is not wanted, and a pleased-sounding 'Good boy' or 'There' or whatever you choose, to indicate your pleasure. Despite the fact that horses do not use the same vocal system as us, it is amazing how quickly they understand these words, as if by instinct, and come to associate them appropriately. Let's just be thankful for it.

Of course, you must give a young horse absolutely no cause whatsoever for complaint. All his equipment must be comfortable and correctly fitted and adjusted. You must behave correctly and responsibly and you must not ask of him anything for which he has not been prepared, as he will have no chance of doing it. 'Naughtiness' or objection from him then is perfectly reasonable.

## A TRAINING SCHEDULE

Many entire, fully detailed and excellent books have been written on the subject of bringing up young horses to the 'riding away' stage – where they can be ridden off the lunge and be reasonably well-behaved, familiar with vocal commands and physical aids because of their lunge and long-rein work. The following, very potted, schedule is intended to give readers an idea of what horses can be fairly expected to do at what ages.

*At all times, handlers should remain calm and quiet, firm but not harsh, and with a positive attitude.*

### The Day after Birth Onwards

The foal should start to be accustomed to handling by humans. The mare should be held in case she is very protective and, keeping the foal next to his dam, a soft, well-fitting foal slip (initial headcollar) should be fitted and the foal introduced to the preliminaries of leading in hand. Use stable rubbers or old tea towels around the foal's hindquarters and lower neck, and one handler at each end, to guide him firmly but softly, next to his dam, around the loosebox and, over the coming days, out to a small exercise area. The handler at the forehand can hold the rubber round the base of his neck and the rope from the slip, and the handler at the hindquarters holds the rubber round the quarters whilst a third handler leads the dam. Never get between the foal and his dam at this stage. In this way, the foal is controlled effectively but safely and reassuringly.

As he starts moving, say 'Walk on' and as he stops say 'Stand' so that he associates these movements with the vocal commands. Soon, he will obey the commands, and one handler can lead the foal from his rope and

It is far better to start educating youngsters from very early in life, even just by getting them used to being handled and directed and, very importantly, letting them investigate the world and broaden their minds. When serious work begins, they learn much quicker if they are already experienced and socialized.

the neck rubber, using a hand behind the hindquarters if forward impetus is needed. Another handler leads the mare. Eventually, the rubber can be dispensed with and ultimately one handler can lead both mare and foal. When being turned out, both mare and foal should turn to face the gate before release (foal first, instantly followed by dam) so that the foal does not learn, or the mare resume, the dangerous and difficult habit of running off into the paddock. When bringing in, catch the mare first, then the foal.

Getting foals used to basic, daily handling is much easier with young animals who can take their example from their dam and are not so strong and resistant as they would be if left for a few months – or even years. Feet need checking and maybe trimming every few weeks to ensure straight action through to maturity, so it is no good waiting until the youngster is a stronger, semi-wild weanling.

The foal should be accustomed gradually to having his feet picked up and then gently tapped to prepare him for his first farriery visit at a few weeks old, to check development, conformation and action. By 6 months of age he should be leading politely, obeying simple, consistent commands, be easy to catch, be willing to be stroked and gently brushed all over and, in general, a pleasure to be with.

## Weaning

If specifically carried out, this should not normally occur before 6 months of age, and preferably 8 months. The weanling should be kept with others of similar age *and* with mature horses to act as disciplinary influences. These two factors help to ensure some level of normal psychological development and sociability under a highly artificial weaning system. Peer 'discipline' alone is not sufficient. Handling should continue and the weanling can be led about the premises with an older, familiar horse (maybe being reintroduced to his dam after she has dried up) and allowed to experience all the sights, sounds and smells. Two well-behaved weanlings could be led around together. If, from their earliest days, they can watch other horses being ridden, it does seem to help them when the time comes for them to be backed. Depending on the weather, they can be introduced to rugs during their first winter.

## Yearlings

Yearlings should lead well in hand, be well-used to having their feet handled by attendants and farrier, move over and stand still in the stable, as required, be used to stable and turnout rugs (if used), be easy to turn out and catch and maybe travel well. They should be used to being groomed and maybe trimmed (kindly). They should be fairly well-disciplined and know that treating humans like horses is definitely not allowed – no kicking, biting, pushing, shoving, striking out, trampling on or playing with. The humans should realize this, as well, and not permit it simply on the grounds that 'Youngsters don't know any better', or 'are only playing'.

## Two-year-olds

At this age, horses should be behaving beautifully in all respects (except for actual work, with which they can now start to be familiarized). Some people introduce a comfortable bit before this age, plus loose side-reins, especially for colts, but many leave it until now, or later. Before starting work, the youngster's legs should be protected with well-fitting and comfortable brushing-cum-tendon boots put on over a soft layer of Gamgee. Some people also like to fit overreach or bell boots at this stage, too, but make sure that they are not too long or they will irritate, rub and trip him.

The youngster can be taught to long-rein in walk for short periods (even just 10 minutes at the very start, progressing to 20 including frequent breaks) but should not be put into any kind of outline. He will be finding his balance in his working gear and that is enough for now. Initially, there should be one handler at the head to lead in a familiar way and one long-reining behind, for as many weeks or months as necessary. It is best initially to attach the long-reins to the side rings of a strong, stable and comfortable lungeing cavesson, not to a bit at this age, in my view. The leader can clip the rope (preferably a long lead or half-length lungeing rein) to the front ring of the cavesson and carry a schooling whip with which to touch the horse appropriately to back up the trainer's vocal commands, should he not respond.

Some breeders and producers start letting horses of this age pop over very low, safe obstacles – no more than logs on the ground or little jumps up to about one foot (30 cm) in height. Others make their horses jump much higher than this but, even on good, yielding (not deep) going, I feel that this is placing too much stress on legs and backs and does not make for a sound horse with a long career ahead of him. The consequences of such practice can be compounded by the fact that virtually all young horses jump unnecessarily high, so a youngster asked to jump, say, 2ft 6 in (76 cm) will probably jump well over 3 ft (90 cm) – perhaps higher. Apart from producing physical strain, this tendency to jump too high also makes the youngster susceptible to being over-faced and becoming fearful of jumping.

## Three-year-olds

At this age, horses can start their formal training, but if they have been well brought up, are leading very well, maybe long-reining, obeying commands and behaving in all respects like a socialized, well-mannered young horse, the process is just a continuation of the preliminary education. Lungeing is still a staple means of educating horses but be sure that it is carried out calmly for very short periods at first on large circles, almost to the end of the lunge line and with no coercive gadgetry. Circles are demanding for horses and small ones are too much to ask of green youngsters.

## Four-year-olds

Four-year-olds can continue with a regime including lungeing and long-reining, becoming more and more proficient, and do hour-long hacks and 40 minutes maximum schooling, with very frequent breaks standing or walking on a loose rein. They can start ridden showing classes as 4-year-olds but should not be given long, wearying days. At this age, horses can go hunting and do other activities, as well, but the main point to remember is that the days must be short and I would certainly give them a day off, ideally with friends in the paddock, the next day.

Generally, 4-year-olds should be going well for their age under saddle, not being held or forced in at the front, nor asked to start getting their weight on to their hindquarters. The muscles of the hindquarters and hind legs need time to grow, develop and strengthen, but a correct way of going for their level of training is essential so as to promote this development and get the horse going habitually in a horizontal balance.

## Five-year-olds

Five-year-olds can begin light 'adult' work. This is the age when they often begin to be over-faced, even though they may have been tenderly handled previously. People often think that, because horses have a full mouth of permanent teeth by this time, they are physically mature – but they are not, and they are not mentally mature either. They can be given short days out working or competing at whatever level they have achieved at home – or preferably a slightly easier level.

By now, if they have been ridden and schooled correctly, they should be able to start taking more weight on their hindquarters and working towards collection by working from 'back to front', as it is often described. The biggest mistake to make as far as the horse's riding and schooling is concerned is to use the hands or training aids inappropriately to bring in the head and lift and probably 'shorten' the neck. What actually needs to happen is for the horse to start to lower his quarters a little more and take more weight on to them. For this, he needs to have been given the time to build up strength in his hindquarters and hind legs, which is done by correct work for his age over a couple of years. This will not be achieved simply by pulling in the head and lifting the neck by means of the hands or equipment.

## OTHER PROGRESSIONS

As stated earlier, the schedule given is for general guidance: there may be perfectly good grounds for varying it somewhat in individual cases. However, major departures should be treated with caution, for reasons outlined briefly below.

### Starting Young

Some years ago, I remember some studies being done which appeared to show that bringing young Thoroughbreds into careful and reasonable work as 2-year-olds actually toughened up their legs and probably made for a sounder future. A common problem in young Thoroughbreds is sore or 'bucked' shins, usually involving tiny fractures of the front surface of the cannon bones of mainly the forelegs, caused by overwork, especially on firm ground. A lot of training and racing days are lost because of this problem. If their work could be modified to avoid it and keep the youngsters sound, it could possibly enhance the youngsters' future physical strength.

The major drawback to putting out this information to the general public would be that 2-year-olds of all kinds might be put to work with far less skill and expertise than that needed to ensure their correct development and soundness. I am certainly still against backing and/or significantly working horses below the age of 3 years and hope the trend to work potential competition horses too young can be stopped. Interestingly, it seems to be the field of racing (in Europe, at any rate), where one might expect the greatest financial pressures, that is leading the way in working young horses less. That is to say, although the precocious Thoroughbred continues to be raced at 2 years of age, many trainers are 'backing off' and running their two-year-olds less frequently than used to be the case.

### Leaving it Late

The other side of the coin is when horses do not start work until they are mature. Again, in some quarters, fillies from valued bloodlines often start breeding at a young age before they have been backed, ridden and proven as performance horses. Colts, too, may be be given basic leading and handling training and then used at stud for a few years, before being gelded, backed, schooled and competed.

I find that some horses in this category can pose quite significant problems to their future owners because, despite having been disciplined, backed and schooled to a high enough standard to make them saleable commodities as riding horses, they never quite, in my experience, come completely to hand. Their minds have matured along with their bodies, they have developed a fairly independent mindset and they often do not take entirely kindly to working. There are obviously many exceptions but I have come across too many of them for it to be a fluke, particularly with entires gelded late.

The best way to proceed does seem to be along the lines of the age/timeline given earlier. This gives youngsters basic discipline from Day 2, progressing and increasing throughout the horse's young years, and it has been proved time and time again to produce well-mannered, well-made horses at maturity, if the job is done properly. This does not mean that young or even older 'renegades' cannot be brought to hand, but it is always easier, as with other animals and children, to start young and keep the lid on any tendency towards bad behaviour as they attempt to kick over the traces while they grow up. Animals and people alike recognize and thrive on fair, firm discipline, but all suffer and are spoiled by too much stress, demands that are too heavy, and harsh methods.

CHAPTER 3

# The Effect of the Herd

I f there is one fact that all 'thinking' trainers and handlers know and work with, it is that horses are herd animals. Surprisingly, not everyone has that at the forefront of their mind, but if you do it makes your job and your horse's life with humans much easier.

## HOW HORSES LEARN IN THEIR NATURAL STATE

The main points about life in a herd and the learning process are that horses learn from birth from their elders and peers what behaviour is acceptable to other herd members and what is not, and they also learn the way to survive in their environment by watching and following their herd (initially, their dams).

So, not only do they learn how to survive in a herd and remain accepted by other horses who are mainly their own families, but also how to survive in their environment – which includes where to find food, water and shelter and how to spot and 'read' predators. (Not all predators are hunting all the time: they behave differently when they are hunting from when they are not.)

Because of the exposed nature of their lifestyle on grassland, horses cannot normally hide from danger. Their first line of defence is flight and, even then, they have to keep a safe distance between themselves and the predators in order to stand a good chance of escaping by sheer speed. As

Horses brought up in the company of as naturally structured a herd as possible have much better manners with humans than those brought up more artificially, say with no others of their own age, not allowed to run in a crowd and learn natural manners, and not allowed sufficient liberty and space to grow strong and agile. The horse on the left is clearly telling the one on the right to clear off, and he has taken the hint – but not before he has received a meaningful bite on his bottom.

mentioned in the first chapter, in order to assess a situation, horses have evolved to be extremely perceptive and able to judge even small changes in their environment and in the demeanour, postures and actions both of other horses and other animals including, of course, humans.

In a herd, a foal learns first from his dam. If she is a good mother, she will let him drink when he needs to, will protect him from the attentions of others (although increasingly less so as he matures) and will seek him out if he wanders too far away. The foal normally learns within 24 hours how to get up and lie down, how to suckle for milk and how to manage four very long, gangly legs to keep up with his dam, even at fast gaits. His senses improve as he matures and he automatically picks up the significance of sounds, smells and tastes. His own sight and his dam's reactions to various situations teach him what they mean and he is soon able to make his own associations with different circumstances.

## Natural Parameters

With regard to how this relates to being ridden, horses learn in the herd that they cannot have all their own way. They probably have the instinct to need the company of other horses, but those other horses will not be as tolerant as their dams. If a youngster does something to another horse which the latter does not like, he may well receive a bite or a kick to tell him to go away. He learns effectively that the action he perpetrated on the other horse is not acceptable. He will also learn which horses accept what behaviour and he will, as he grows up, learn that by using the same gestures and actions, he, too, can to tell other horses what he will put up with and from whom – and what he will not tolerate. Not for nothing is 'horseplay' noted for being rough, but it is not usually seriously injurious. That is not to say that horses 'making a point' are gentle with each other. A meaningful bite from a horse's incisors hurts another horse as much as it hurts us. In fact, some say that the pain threshold of horses is lower than that of humans.

The young horse also learns the signs to give which indicate that he does not mean harm when approaching another horse, particularly a senior one. He learns to gauge another horse's emotions, state or intentions by observing body language – and he learns to do this with predators and people, too.

## LEARNING TO INTERACT WITH HUMANS

All that has been described is essential learning to a young horse in a herd situation, and horses apply the same criteria to humans for, in domesticity, humans are, in a way, part of the horse's herd, even though they are obviously aware that we are not horses. Horses from a well-run stud who have learnt from their earliest days, painlessly, that humans are invincible because they have methods of control and manipulation which are irresistible, are understandably much easier to live with and school than those who have not been well brought up as foals and/or have been subjected to unfair dominance and pain in other hands. The latter learn naturally to defend themselves against this sort of treatment and may well learn that they can win, after all, and join the ranks of spoilt, difficult and dangerous horses which seem to be increasing owing to lack of natural-style discipline and logical, fair training.

Most people do not have their horses from foal-hood, or even youth. There are many more mature horses than young ones and many of those go the rounds from owner to owner because they do not behave as the new owner requires, or has been led to expect by the seller. They have 'bad habits', in our terms, but the horse is only behaving as he has learnt to do from experience, from formed habits, from possibly trying to work out what different owners mean and from trying to defend himself against confusion, distress, discomfort and pain.

## Horses Don't Forget, but can Relearn

A horse presenting his owner with problems is behaving in the way life has taught him, by association of ideas and the formation of habits. The good news is that 'bad' behaviour can be improved a great deal by creating good associations for the horse with a particular task or situation.

For instance, imagine you have a horse who shakes with fear or backs into the far corner of his stable every time he sees someone coming towards him with a saddle. He is associating the act of being saddled up with discomfort, pain and other distressing things but, if he can be fed tasty titbits every time someone approaches him with a saddle, progressing to being fed them as the saddle is put on very gently, he can come to associate being saddled up with good things and will submit willingly. The same principle applies to most things we need to do to horses, from basic handling, being shod, having injections, tacking-up and so on.

When it comes to riding, it is necessary to have accustomed the horse to hearing a sound which tells him that all is well and you are happy and calm (which is what the horse, as a prey and herd animal, wants you to be). Hunting predators are not happy and calm. They exude tension and determination. Angry herd members can also spell danger, so horses naturally prefer to avoid both. An injured horse is at risk of being killed and eaten because predators pick out the weakest and easiest to kill, therefore, the horse's main instinctive aim is to stay functional and healthy.

The reason why you need to bring a sound into the association is because you cannot consistently deliver food rewards from the saddle within the second it takes for the horse to associate it with whatever he has just done. Delivering the goody later does not form the association: the horse may enjoy it and it makes the rider feel good, but the opportunity for creating the link has been missed. Most people use the word or words 'Good' or 'Good boy/girl' but it can be any pleased, calm-sounding word (such as 'Yes' or 'There'). Initially, at the instant you give a treat, say the word. The horse then links the word, the treat and the action, so very soon you can just use the word from the saddle to let the horse know that he has just done something that makes you happy. A special little stroke on the withers can be used as well, or instead. The point is that you must be consistent and within the timeframe (which is usually held to be within a second, two at the very most) for the horse to make the association.

How about telling the horse that he is 'wrong', though, and has just done something which does *not* make you happy? Because horses are very sensitive to the tone of the human voice, this is not difficult. When he has done something you don't want, just say (not shout) 'No' sternly and, if possible, use firm but painless physical means to correct the horse – this is easy with a young foal, of course, but not with a bigger, stronger animal – which is why it's best to start from Day 2 (the first 24 hours being left mainly for the mare and foal to form their bond).

If, for instance, the horse has just moved from where you have placed him with the word 'Stand' (which you are certain he understands), *as* he moves say 'No' sternly and immediately physically put him back where he was, then repeat the command, 'Stand'. If he moves again say 'No' and repeat; if he stands say 'Good boy' or whatever you have chosen and maybe give a titbit *at the same time.*

(The horse should, of course, have been taught the command 'Stand' in hand as a youngster, or at least on the lunge and long-reins. However, if he does not understand it, every time he comes to a halt say 'Stand' as he does so, then 'Good boy' and treat him. He will soon associate standing still with the command and with pleasure. Pretty soon, you will just be able to say 'Stand' and he will do so. In fact, many horses will reach the point where, as soon as they hear the 'S' sound, they will stand still, so all you have to do is give a little hiss and there you are.)

That is the basic principle of teaching obedience to words or sounds, and to aids. As the horse performs the act you want, give the command at that very instant and say your praise word, giving the treat very quickly afterwards. The praise word is known as the 'bridge' between correct action and treat – it lets the horse know that the treat is coming if, for some reason, you cannot give it instantaneously.

With a problematical horse, this is the way to swap bad associations for good ones. Be aware, though, that the bad memories/associations will remain in the horse's brain and, if the circumstances recur which triggered them in the first place, such as a brutal trainer, a rough farrier, a sound or smell association, or an accident entering transport, the previous behaviour *may* surface again.

Of course, you cannot go through your horse's life giving him treats every time he does something right but, with established, learnt moves, using praise words and actions such as particular strokes tells him that you are happy, calm (even if you aren't) and pleased.

## Pressure

Just like us, horses can enjoy pressure or dislike or fear it. It all depends on the type of pressure.

A short, sharp, intermittent and maybe repetitive pressure like a horse being bitten or kicked by another has a rejecting quality which clearly means 'go away', whereas a sustained rubbing, massaging or nuzzling kind of feeling gives pleasure, like horses giving each other mutual grooming with their very muscular and mobile top lips, or their upper incisors. Mutual grooming is thought to be important in strengthening bonds, friendships and general ties with 'preferred associates' or friends and favoured family members.

These two quite different types of pressure – intermittent and sustained

Horses naturally resist or lean into sustained pressure, as can be seen here, but move away from intermittent pressure, such as a bite as shown in the previous photo (page 62) or, when accustomed to it, a gentle tap or touch on the side from our hand. This is an important way in which we can use their natural inclinations in schooling, as good, logical application of the aids consists of releasing the pressure (aid) the instant the horse obeys.

– are reacted to by horses in different and appropriate ways. Few horses would stand around to be bitten or kicked and normally move off unless a fight or serious fracas is in progress and they are giving as good as they get. On the other hand, mutual grooming, friendly nuzzling and such contact as grazing with bodies touching, as friends do, are enjoyed and horses usually lean into this type of sustained pressure quite naturally. From the point of view of giving aids and handling horses generally, these two different, natural reactions by horses to pressure are very useful for us.

To give a horse an enjoyable feeling, calm him down, reassure him or give him a good association with something he has just done (a 'reward' – although the horse may not see it that way), we can firmly stroke his withers, the lower part of his neck nearest his shoulders, or the shoulders themselves. These are the areas most often mutually groomed by horses and, conveniently, are easily reached from the saddle or when standing by a horse's head. On the other hand, the wild, delighted and obviously thoughtless thumping which many poor horses receive from their riders when they have just done well in a competition will be naturally interpreted as a rejecting, unpleasant action like biting and kicking – quite the opposite action from that which makes a horse feel good.

Sustained pressure as an aid can certainly be misused. Constant bit pressure via the reins is actually believed to be good and necessary by some, but this often results in a horse's head and neck being restricted (even if the pressure is firm but not actually harsh), so he cannot move them at all naturally to help him balance or move freely. Many riders, in my experience, actually and clearly have a very significant, sustained contact on their horse's mouth and are holding the head and neck in what can only be described as a vice-like grip, perhaps in the (genuine but mistaken) belief that they are 'supporting' the horse with the bit to assist his balance and 'help' him to adopt the correct posture or outline. They claim that this is necessary in order to teach the horse to go habitually in that posture and to develop the muscles throughout his body correctly (for riding), so that he will be able to work safely in the way required whilst bearing weight.

While there may be a certain rationale to this thought process, I feel it is fatally flawed. Ethically, it is extremely unpleasant and often clearly distressing for the horse – not at all horse-friendly. Horses ridden in this way are preoccupied with avoiding the considerable discomfort (maybe pain) of such a contact and show their distress by their tense facial expressions, distorted muzzles, seemingly shortened or 'squashed-in' necks and excessive frothing and salivation. In terms of biomechanics this type of contact – from firm to heavy – does not, in practice, 'support' the horse, 'help' him, or 'assist his balance'. In fact, it greatly hinders him.

When you get on such horses and ride them in a classical, light and horse-friendly way, in my experience as a rider, trainer and teacher, they are without exception actually incapable of balancing themselves properly. It takes differing amounts of time, in minutes, for individuals to 'find their feet' and realize that they can actually move in the outline or frame their rider is indicating whilst being given the necessary and natural facility of their balancing pole – their head and neck – and, therefore, the freedom to move comfortably, joyfully and correctly in self-balance. Relieved of the awful pressure in their mouths, their minds are no longer looking for ways to avoid it or work round it but can concentrate on their new-found freedom to enjoy their work.

When deprived of this beneficial facility, they strain their bodies against the handicap of a fixed head and neck and, although they do develop impressive-looking musculature, (probably in the wrong places) many of them actually appear muscle-bound rather than possessing the sleek, rounded and healthier-looking development of a horse trained in the methods of lightness with self-control. In human terms, it is the difference between the appearance of a weight-lifter and a gymnast or dancer. Which is the more agile?

The converse of the over-restrictive contact is a light, mainly sustained contact with the outside rein and a lighter inside rein giving intermittent aids as required to produce a sensitive, made mouth, which truly can be used for two-way communication rather than one-way coercion.

Sustained pressure of the legs against the horse's sides is also counter-productive as it makes truly light leg aids impossible and dulls the horse's sides. Legs which are draped down and round the ribcage and belly are in touch but not pressing on. Then, when the rider gives an intermittent, on-off aid with one or both legs, repeating as necessary, the horse knows that something is wanted, moves accordingly and the aid stops, or should do. Intermittent pressure, to a horse, means 'go away', 'move' (away from the pressure). Of course, when ridden, the horse cannot move away from the rider but can move away from the leg (maybe sideways or forwards) and relieve himself of its intermittent tapping or squeezing.

One of the most pointless things unskilled riders do is grind upwards with the heels and keep the pressure on the horse's sides, maintaining the (sustained and maybe increasing) pressure until he moves. This often causes sluggish movement and, not being a light, quick aid, creates a dull horse. Combined with a very firm rein contact (which basically means 'stop' or 'slow down' to a barely schooled horse), such 'aids' clearly do not put the rider on the path to lightness and responsive, free, forward movement.

These matters are discussed further in the next chapter.

## From Ground to Saddle

So long as the horse is being led in hand or lunged, he sees himself as having company, albeit human. When horses are long-reined, the human company may not always be visible if walking or running directly behind the horse (and a helper leading the horse has been dispensed with), but the trainer can always move just a little to one side or the other, and thus step into the horse's range of almost all-round vision.

Once the horse is backed and 'riding away' without a handler at his head or walking near him, the company he would always have in a herd, and has had in human form until now, is apparently 'absent' and he may well suddenly feel alone and hesitant. This is why the verbal commands must be thoroughly instilled into him, and it should be becoming second nature to him to obey them and link or associate them with physical aids (bit and legs) before this stage is reached. Without this verbal back-up, the rider is lacking a valuable means of reassuring and communicating with the horse and, indeed, is at a disadvantage when it comes to actual control. Deprived of his 'herd' (a human in view) and probably with no equine company, either, it will be no wonder if he becomes afraid, confused, worried and not inclined to obey his rider. However, if plenty of time has been taken over the 'transfer' stage, problems are much less likely to arise.

The job of getting the horse to obey physical, ridden aids is, again, achieved by means of the association of ideas and experiences. As stated earlier, this book is not specifically about backing or starting and riding away youngsters – there are many excellent books

Although, ultimately, horses should learn to work alone and regard their rider as their companion, using an experienced, reliable horse to lead a young or uncertain one through tricky places and over obstacles is an excellent, tried and tested method of giving the latter both confidence and a smooth passage through his lessons.

on that speciality – but the basic procedure might run as follows.

The horse has learnt his basic human vocabulary in hand, on the lunge and maybe on long-reins and so understands 'Walk on', 'Terr-ot', 'Trot on' or 'Trotting' (choose one for trot and stick with it as they all sound different to the horse) and 'Can-ter', plus 'Stand', 'Back' and 'Over'. He needs to be very familiar with these sounds and reliably and habitually co-operating with them so that he can clearly associate the new aids under saddle with the same sounds and movements.

The horse will have been accustomed to a saddle also, and to a lightweight person lying over it (or just over his bare back, according to preference), then putting a leg across and keeping their upper body low over his withers whilst stroking (not patting) him. At this point, the youngster's familiar trainer talks reassuringly, using words he knows such as 'Good boy'. The 'rider' can gradually sit up and remain completely passive and quiet, not gripping with legs or seat whilst the trainer leads them around in a safe, enclosed area, using words the horse now obeys readily – 'Walk on' and 'Stand'. This should be done for about 10 or 15 minutes most days until the horse takes it all for granted.

(Horses vary in the time they take to reach this stage, but should be watched carefully for their reactions and not rushed at all. I do realize that there are many other, quicker methods of backing and riding away horses – of any age – but still maintain that rushing the process is not good for the horse's attitude or spirit in the long run and, therefore, for his future relationship with and trust of people. I have seen many horses started off quickly, sometimes extremely quickly, and feel that they all seem to have a zombie-like, shell-shocked air about them which I wouldn't want in *my* horses.)

When the horse is quite at home with all this, the process can be continued in a safe area, either indoors or out. At first, continue with leading, stopping and starting, using consistently familiar words and pressures on his headgear. At this stage, he can simply wear a good lungeing cavesson with reins attached to the side rings and the lead rope (a long one half the length of a lungeing rein) attached to the nose ring. Later, a bridle and bit (no noseband) can be fitted under the cavesson with the cheekpieces brought out over the cavesson's noseband. The trainer still has the lead rope clipped to the front ring and the rider has the reins, now attached to the bit.

From halt, the trainer says 'Walk on' and moves into walk. *At the very instant the horse moves forward,* the rider gives one gentle on-off squeeze with the legs so that the horse associates the feeling or aid with moving forward. To halt, the trainer slows and says 'Stand' and *the instant the horse slows* the rider gives gentle on-off pressure on the bit. In this way, again, the horse learns to associate the rider's aid with the movement. Please note that:

- *Initially, in the learning phase, it is absolutely crucial to give the aid the moment the horse does what's wanted so that the two go together and the association or link between the two can be made in his brain. The rider then sits passively again.*
- *The trainer and rider use their judgement as to how well the horse is grasping this concept (it's his natural way of learning, anyway) so that, at the correct stage, the rider can just give the physical aid and the trainer ceases to use the voice. At that point, it is just as crucial, once the horse is obeying the physical aid alone, to stop the aid the instant he complies. This is his confirmation that he has acted as you wish. If you keep on giving the aid to (in your mind) make him walk on more, he cannot make the association and will become confused.*

This is a simple outline of how all training progresses. Of course, as horses become more advanced, aids can be reduced to mere nuances of 'feel' and such things as weight and position aids are added to his vocabulary. Horses in a learning environment become absorbed in their lessons and, I am sure, know very well that we are teaching them things, not just randomly doing things to them. They react as nature equipped them to do and the better we understand their learning process the more successful and horse-friendly will our schooling and riding be.

Some particularly good books on this huge subject are listed at the end of this book under Further Reading.

# CHAPTER 4

# The Rider's Responsibility

For most people, the world has never been an easy place in which to live. When we look back at past ages it must have been even tougher than it is now, but in many different ways. Few of us would want to go back to living without easy means of heating, transport, acquiring food and so on, not to mention medical and dental care and, wonder of wonders, effective anaesthetics and pain-killers but, of course, our planet is paying the price for many aspects of our modern lifestyles.

Horses have been domesticated for about 6,000 years and life has never been easy for them, either. Wild and feral horses are constantly at the mercy of illness and injury, the weather and predatory creatures, both insect predators and other mammals. Domestic horses, depending on their owners, have the advantages of veterinary and dental care and a ready food supply, shelter, no predation and longer lives. In the past, most working horses had short and often very hard lives as we used them for transport and war. Today, developed countries do not need horses for transport and war; they are not essential to our society and are used largely as a source of pleasure for us for riding, driving and the various equestrian sports.

Unfortunately, it is clear that the rise in the popularity of equestrian competition has attracted certain people who only own horses and ride in order to compete, or to take part in some other activity for which a horse is needed. This means that the horse's needs are often not a top priority with the owner. As with the ubiquitous and essential working horse of times past, if the horse cannot do the job, he is out. Many owners feel that there is nothing wrong with this, and that, so long as they look after the horse while they own him, they have done right by him. This is certainly better than being what I call a *horse-user* – someone who treats the horse as little better than a machine and has virtually no feeling for him as a living, sentient fellow creature. Worse than this are those who buy horses just to have something impressive to possess and make them look good, and worst of all are those who have them because they want something to dominate and make them appear powerful because they can control an animal as big and strong as a horse.

The ideal situation for the horse, of course, is to have an owner who is deeply interested in forming a partnership with their horse or horses, based on real caring and acceptance of responsibility for the welfare and well-being of a living creature with needs and feelings. The fact that the horse may be able to do something for the owner in the form of being ridden comes second to the partnership and to the fact that the horse is absolutely dependent on the owner for everything, right up to a humane end when the time comes.

Those who keep horses on this basis and have been fortunate enough to develop a close relationship and friendship with them rarely part with their horses – and then only if they become utterly unable to keep them. (However, as in poor interpersonal relationships, there are occasions when a horse and his owner simply do not 'get on' and then the fairest thing for the horse is to try to find a suitable new owner for him: this is dealt with in Chapter 12.) Where a horse does not have the aptitude for the rider's preferred activity or activities, it seems that too many people try for too long to 'make' the horse fit the role they want, such as jumping, dressage or whatever, because they think that 'failure' to do so reflects on them. However, in such cases it is much more sensible to acknowledge that the horse is not cut out for the intended role and find him a decent home doing what he *is* good at.

## ATTITUDE

In an age when good manners and consideration for others are not taught to many people as a matter of course, so the traditional horseman's or horsewoman's attitude of real consideration for the horse, and of putting him first, is also scarcer than in the past.

The attitude which a committed, concerned horse owner or rider needs,

An impressive display of tactful riding and trust between horse and rider. Riding without a bridle is not at all new but requires sound, rational schooling aimed at giving the horse enjoyment and confidence.

and may well have naturally, is just as described above. Such a person will care genuinely for their own (and others') horses and, no matter what is on the agenda, will not do anything which is likely to result in distress or harm to them. Contrary to the opinions of some, horses do have emotions and also feel discomfort and pain just as we do, so these facts must be taken into account when planning their lives.

A good owner will also take every opportunity to learn as much as is reasonably possible about horse care and management, riding and schooling, psychology and behaviour. For many, this is not seen as a chore or duty but is a deep, abiding interest.

Advances in veterinary knowledge and equine science, especially, occur regularly and we need to be up to date on this score. It is important, for the horse's sake, not to refuse to learn, or to let other people make your decisions for you, however expert and persuasive they may be. Learn as much as you can. Think about and look into the actual merits of new schools of thought, discoveries, advances and developments yourself, and examine the advice you are given. Ask around and do your own research so that you can come to an informed decision, using your knowledge and your common sense, on the best course of action for your particular horse.

# TECHNIQUE

One of the basic requirements of a good rider is an independent seat and hands. This means that you do not need, or feel the inclination, to use the reins via your hands to help you to stay in position or actually remain on your horse. It also means that you can use your hands independently of each other but also, most importantly, independently of your body, so that you only use the amount and type of contact needed to communicate with your horse. A rider who does not have independent body balance and security unavoidably makes movements which create pressures on the horse's mouth and neck (via the bit and reins respectively) which have nothing to do with communication, but simply with staying put in the saddle. This is not what the hands, reins and bit are for: they are for communication only.

In order to reach this necessary state for horse-friendly riding, you have to take the time and make the effort to develop an independent seat, so that your seat itself is secure in the saddle and you don't need to use your hands to try to stay on. The best way to do this, in practice, is to work without reins and stirrups on the lunge and over grids and little jumps. By these means, you can learn to develop your balance and co-ordination in the saddle, learning to sit into the horse with a toned, deep (but not heavy) and secure seat. If you do not have a deep seat and your legs are stiff, and if you do not have good upper body posture (being inclined to lean back or crouch forwards), gripping with your legs will raise you up out of the saddle and *reduce* your security. In emergencies, gripping with your legs *in conjunction with* a deep seat and correct upper body posture will *add* to your security.

I teach all my clients to drop their 'awareness' down into their centre (inside the abdomen just below the navel and just above the seat bones) and to 'think with their seat'. This immediately 'lightens' their heads and upper bodies so that they are no longer top-heavy, frees the hands and creates a much closer contact between the centres of gravity of both rider and horse. The overall effect is a secure, moulded seat which gives the horse most of his direction – exactly what you and he want.

# HORSEMANSHIP

To the term 'horseman', coined at a time when virtually all riders were male, we can add the equivalent 'horsewoman', both forms conveying much more than a mere 'rider'. There are many qualities of a true horseman/woman, some of which are calmness at all times, well-judged firmness, kindness, sensitivity, gentleness, confidence, fairness, real knowledge, open-mindedness and a bright, positive outlook on life. I am sure readers can think of others.

A horseman or woman is, first and foremost, a 'thinking' person with a very well developed sense of integrity. He or she does not take anything for granted, least of all the horse's health, behaviour or well-being. Whether or not such a person competes or takes part in other mounted sports, personal enjoyment or the kudos of winning prizes is never put before the horse's welfare. Sometimes, in competitive situations, people are pressured to remember their 'duty' to the team, or their country, in ways that might compromise the horse's welfare. However, in the context of sporting endeavour, this is unacceptable and a true horseman or woman will always put their horse's interests first.

Horses thrive in a settled environment and in the care of people they can trust and rely on to do the right thing by them – even though they may not think of it in quite those terms. They can behave quite differently under a different regime: they know the difference between a horseman/woman and a 'user' and react according to their temperament. Some become aggressive, others appear stubborn, and some develop 'stable vices' (stereotypical behaviours) from frustration and anxiety, while others become withdrawn and miserable.

Horsemen and women may be born with their natural inclinations and qualities intact, but they can also be made by means of educating, feeding and stretching an open, absorptive mind.

## EQUINE PERSONALITIES

Like humans and other animals, horses have different personalities and character traits which determine how they react to different circumstances and situations. In this respect, getting to know and being able to 'read' a horse is very much like doing the same with any other animal, a child or a fellow adult. Briefly, below are a few equine personality types and ideas about how to deal with them. It should be remembered that whenever you are having problems with a horse you first need to check that he has no physical problems causing him discomfort, ranging from lameness or physical soreness to badly fitting tack and sharp teeth. Horses often work a good deal on memories of what has happened to them in the past, too, but with consistently good handling, riding and re-schooling, these memories are often overcome.

## Reticent

Horses who are a bit 'backward at coming forward' psychologically need confident, kind and encouraging handling and riding. Don't mistake them for lazy or nervous horses. They may not always answer your aids as promptly as you would wish, either on the ground or from the saddle, but this is because they are perhaps a little unsure about what you are asking them to do, or where you are asking them to go. They may not wish to work in the presence of a domineering or superior horse. You need to assess what situations seem to put them off (location, company, work involved or handlers/riders) so that you can encourage and support them accordingly. Treat them very confidently in an upbeat way, being very ready with praise. With such horses – even more so than others – it is *extremely* important to build confidence in themselves and their surroundings.

## Timid

Timid horses are similar to reticent ones but need very tactful, understanding handling. A confident attitude on your part is essential to give them something to trust and rely on, so that they feel comfortable following your lead. You need to be the strong, quiet type, because if they find anything in your demeanour which raises their levels of nervousness (either lack of confidence or a brash attitude) they will become more set in their ways and the situation could result in defensive and even violent behaviour on their part.

## Domineering

Bossy horses may be just that, or actual bullies. Weak riders and handlers will get walked over (maybe as a matter of fact), and whip-happy handlers can make them actually vicious. They do need very strong, competent but kind and firm people to handle them effectively and safely and they are not suitable or safe for weaker or nervous riders. However, I have known several such horses and ponies go very well for novices and children who did not know what they were like. Non-confrontational handling and riding can certainly work from a rider with the ability to cajole them tactfully into what is wanted.

## Lazy

Some horses appear lazy – but a lot have simply never been taught the forward ethic (see Chapter 8). Many riders mistake speed for going forward but it is not the same thing. 'Forward' means a horse on your aids – one who obeys instantly whether you ask for straight-ahead, sideways or backwards – and who moves at a smart but comfortable speed.

A good way to re-school a 'lazy' horse is on the lunge, with the thong of a lungeing whip snaking behind him, stopping the instant the horse moves. If he does not move, flick out the thong so that the lash just *touches* his thigh without in any way hurting him (practise flicking tin cans off a log with no horses in sight), giving an appropriate command at the same time. When he has caught on, the same command is used by a rider with, if necessary, someone standing nearby with the lunge whip as if the horse were still on the lunge. The penny will drop with the majority of horses and they will develop the habit of going forward. Kicking them at every stride is not the route to go down as this just becomes 'white noise' to them and they learn effectively that it means nothing – certainly not the way to develop light sides and forwardness.

Finally, there are various medical reasons why a horse may appear lethargic and (especially if such an attitude is atypical of the individual) a veterinary check-up may be in order.

## Keen

Riders with 'electric bottoms' are not really suitable for keen horses! What often happens in such a pairing is that the rider almost inevitably starts hanging on to the horse's mouth and/or puts the horse into stronger and stronger bits because they cannot control the energetic response they themselves are, perhaps unwittingly, producing in the horse. A keen horse needs a rider with very quiet seat and legs, kind, reassuring hands on 'reins of silk' and a laid-back 'we're going nowhere' temperament. Calm needs to be the order of every day in the rider in order to try to instil it into the horse.

The energy coming from the horse also needs to be channelled tactfully into the right way of going if he is to develop the correct musculature and not develop the habit of going in a damaging concave shape, which will have the opposite effect. The rider needs to develop the skill of controlling the horse's speed and direction largely with seat, thighs and weight rather than hands. If the last are the main means of speed control, such horses can develop mouth problems – 'hard' or fussy mouths – or become habitually behind the bit and overbent, or else go consistently above the bit and, in either case, be very hard to control.

## Not co-operative

Such horses can make you wonder if there's any point in riding them at all. There is no pleasure in riding and working with a horse who is engaged in a subtle or not-so-subtle battle of wills all the time.

Before riding, you need to check such a horse for comfort, principally teeth, bridle and bit, feet including shoes, and back including saddle, girth and any pads you are using. It is often not realized that much discomfort can be caused unexpectedly by girths digging in behind the elbows, seams and ridges on pads of various sorts pressing on and rubbing, and risers creating uneven pressures on the back or withers. Make certain that all surfaces touching the horse are smooth, even and comfortable.

If you are sure that all is in order and you want to keep working with him, put him through a logical, correct re-schooling programme, emphasizing getting him fully on the aids and habitually obeying your forward aids, because on this hinges his habit of obeying everything else. Also, if your horse does not go truly forward you will effectively go nowhere until he does. Success in this area does benefit everything else, as it affects the horse's mindset. (An action common amongst such horses is that they often try to evade the forward aids by disengaging a hind leg and going crooked. It helps if the rider understands lateral movement and can apply lateral aids quickly, as this can sometimes help 'trump the horse's aces'.)

It also helps to think well ahead of such horses when handling them on the ground. For instance, if you have a horse who tries to block everything you do in his box or the field, try to anticipate what he usually does and take blocking action yourself: if you enter his box and he is facing you, and you make to go to your right and he moves to his left, get hold of his head *first* and gently and firmly push it to his right. If you start grooming his right side and he walks away to his left, walk around his quarters to the left and meet him coming round, then just calmly start grooming his left side, and so on. Of course, you could just tie him up, but that way he will not learn that his tactics don't work.

## *Willing*

It is very easy for the less-than-sensitive owner to overwork such horses and take advantage of their good nature. Whatever you ask them to do, they have a good try at it; they pay attention to you and seem only too happy to go along with your requests. You need to be really perceptive with them to spot the earliest and slightest signs of fatigue, boredom, anxiety, confusion, or not being quite so competent or confident as they give the impression of being. They will still keep trying, so the responsibility is on you to keep their activities within comfortable bounds for them.

## *Confident*

These horses, *provided they are competent as well as confident*, are ideal for nervous and novice riders, who almost always feel as safe as houses on them. Such horses have given many a rider back their 'nerve'. However, problems can arise when such horses are confident in their riders (whoever they may be), and trust their judgement. This can sometimes lead to the rider mistaking confidence for competence in the horse and asking something of which the horse is not really capable, with disastrous results. Over-confidence is a disadvantage in both horse and human, so it is wise to tone down your requests on a horse you do not know very well.

## TRUST

It can take a long time to rebuild the trust of a horse who has had his shattered. Most horses lose their trust in a rider because of abuse to their mouths. As primates, we humans are often far too 'handy' by nature; we use our hands for almost everything including (some of us) trying to keep ourselves in the saddle. The wild movements and harsh pressures this creates in the horse's mouth must be really painful and it is no wonder that so very many horses have mouth problems, which often go unrecognized by their riders.

It can be quite difficult to teach ourselves, and others, to transform human hands into the hands of a horseman/woman – quiet, gentle but firm enough to be reassuring, consistent with their aids and certainly never abusive or a source of confusion, distress or pain. There should be no pulling backwards, no harsh pressure, no aid at all when we are not actively trying to communicate with the horse, and the aids we do give should be the minimum which will get the desired result. As mentioned under the heading Pressure in Chapter 3, I am very much against maintaining a significant, heavy contact which is often done under the guise of 'supporting' a horse, and find the techniques given in Chapter 5 much more effective in producing a happy horse with a light, educated mouth.

Trust is also often broken by brutal use of the whip. Suffering pain and confusion will destroy any horse's trust, and fear of the whip is one of the most difficult things to overcome, even if you only carry a whip for years and never use it. Such habituation techniques as stroking the horse gently with the whip are often recommended but I have never found that they really work with a horse who has learnt (been taught) to really fear the whip. Some hurts can go too deep to be forgotten and abuse at the hands of a whip-happy rider seems to be one of them. However (provided that the horse doesn't exhibit too extreme a response to the removal of a hand), it can help to take whichever the horse thinks is the 'whip hand' off the reins repeatedly, and just use it to stroke his neck or scratch his withers.

Trust is the most precious quality you can create between you and your horse. I believe that it is crucial to do whatever it takes to develop it and, equally, to try your utmost not to do anything to destroy it.

This pair look very happy in each other's company. The rider is going with the horse and has him on a gentle contact, allowing him to balance himself and use his head and neck, with no overbending. The horse is happy to go forward and enjoy his canter.

# CHAPTER 5

# The Aids

The aids can be defined as signals you give to your horse to help him to understand what you want him to do. The emphasis is on the word 'help': that is what 'aid' means. The signals or aids do not *compel* the horse to do anything. Although he has to be taught what they mean, they can be designed to have at least a close relationship to his natural thought processes and movements, making it easier for him to understand and respond to them.

The comparison of riding with ballroom dancing is a very appropriate analogy. In ballroom dancing, when done correctly and well, the man leads and the lady responds and follows – as an art form it works beautifully. The man holds the lady firmly but comfortably in close contact so that he can guide her with his body positions and his hands. A good leader will give a second or two's warning of any specific steps or changes of direction he is going to make and, if his 'aids' are logical, appropriate and well timed, the lady, with even a little experience, finds it easy to follow him and can soon find herself making some, to her, amazing moves and steps. The result can be really exhilarating, the more so the better you become, like most activities.

Another essential requirement in ballroom (or any) dancing is the posture and bearing of the dancers. Slouching and slopping will get you nowhere, either on the dance floor or on a horse. This does not mean that you cannot relax mentally when riding, just that you will both move together better if you hold yourselves properly.

From the lady's point of view, dancing with a man who does not lead is pretty unfulfilling and limiting; nothing brilliant or even good will ever be achieved. In riding, the rider is the 'man' and the horse is the 'lady'. There is no doubt whatsoever that horses go better and feel more relaxed and confident under a good leader in the equine dance partnership. Even if the horse is green, he will perform better, learn quicker and enjoy the activity more if his leader/rider sits correctly, gives reliable and reassuring seat-support and gives logical, appropriate, comfortable and well-timed aids.

When teaching, I often signal a break in the lesson to discuss or explain something and give the horse a rest on a free rein. After this few minutes, horse and rider will be quite relaxed and switched off, which is fine. The phrase I use to start us all off again is: 'Now, sit to attention and he'll come to attention as well.' Riders new to my methods are always amazed when the horse does exactly that *without any contact on the bit* as they resume the seat, position and bearing I have taught them earlier in the lesson. It almost always happens: simply in response to the 'feel' of the correct seat in the rider and, I am sure, the mental intention to start riding again, the horse 'switches on' and waits for an aid. The power of posture!

It is well known how easily horses assess people; their ability to assess other animals in a trice has been their key to survival. They can tell as soon as a rider mounts what kind of rider he or she is. They can tell just by someone's demeanour on the ground whether or not they are 'horsy' – and what kind of horsy, at that. They react accordingly and with reference to their past experience of humans.

As stated earlier, the aids, of themselves, do not compel a horse to do anything, but he can be brought to the stage at which responding to them in the way we wish becomes habitual for him. Horses form habits and routines very easily and, once a way of responding becomes a habit, riding and handling a horse become easier and safer for us – provided that the habitual responses are what we want. Horses learn bad habits (from our point of view) just as quickly and surely as good ones, so if we ride in a way that creates a wrong response this will become a habit, too.

The most important points about aids are that we must use *clear* signals based, as far as possible, on how horses *operate naturally* and that they should be given at the *right time* in the horse's stride and they must be *consistently the same*.

As aids, you can use your voice, your seat and weight, the whole of your legs from hip joints to feet and your arms and hands. These are often called the natural aids. Whips, spurs and martingales have traditionally been termed the artificial aids so, these days, I suppose that not only martingales but the various training aids we now have could be termed artificial aids. I am not concerned with those in this chapter but do want to discuss the natural aids plus whips and spurs.

## HOW WE SEND SIGNALS

Although not strictly an aid, your general demeanour, body posture and bearing are very meaningful to a horse. A quiet, calm, confident and strong persona is reassuring and informative to horses of all temperaments. Timid, highly-strung and nervous horses will be comforted and calmed by it, most will be reassured by it and the more domineering types will not be so inclined to take advantage of such a person.

### *The Voice*

Some mention has already been made of the voice as a means of communicating with a horse, together with the fact that horses are very sensitive to the human voice. Unfortunately, most people do not use the voice anything like enough – often because they do not think about it, but also because it is not allowed in dressage tests (although the Classical Riding Club does permit its subtle use in its tests).

The reason why the voice is not allowed in tests seems to stem from the days when horses in military use would often be ridden on covert night-time operations when silence was essential, so horses had to learn to work from the other aids. Those days are long gone and, because the voice is such a valuable aid, it is time for its use to be allowed in competitive dressage, the only discipline in which it is forbidden.

The need for aids to be consistent applies just as much to the voice as to the 'physical' aids. The same word said in a significantly different way, including in a different accent, can sound quite different and be confusing to a horse – and remember that some horses start to become a little frightened when they are confused. The tone of voice is important, too. A low, quiet tone calms and slows a horse whereas a bright, perky tone is stimulating.

When you are getting a horse used to a particular vocal aid, at first you need to say it *as* he performs the movement so that he associates the two. Later, you can say the word or phrase and he will perform the movement in response, as he does to the physical aids. Try to choose specific and different-sounding words and phrases for each response you want a horse to make, so that they do not sound alike and confuse the horse. I prefer to use one word or phrase for each response. I note, in particular, that people often use two or three different sounds to ask for trot when lungeing – such as 'Terr-ot', 'Trot on', 'Trotting' and so on. To the horse, these sound quite different although many become very good at sorting out, by trial and error, what we want. It is logical and fair schooling, however, not to make a horse play guessing games with you. Try to keep to one word or simple phrase for one movement and your horse will find life easier.

The first thing a horse should learn is his name: I have always wondered why people always teach household pets their names but hardly ever seem to do so with their horses. When a horse knows his name, it is really convenient for getting his attention at any time, for warning him – like a verbal half-halt – that something such as an aid is coming, or to use as you approach his box or go to him, or call him to you, in the field. Many people also use specific sounds to calm, slow down or increase speed or energy. 'Eeeeeasy' is useful for calming; a long drawn-out 'Whoa' seems a natural with most horses for slowing down and tongue clicks are often used for more energy with 'Go on' being used for gallop.

A very useful command on the ground or from the saddle is 'Head down'. Apart from the fact that having the head down calms horses of itself (but not if it is forced), it is useful in helping to cope with head-shy horses and in getting horses to adopt a more correct posture if they are not responding to physical aids. Many horses drop their heads if you just say their name, bend down and point to the ground. You can also do it, of course, by offering a titbit and saying 'Head down' as they lower their heads. Once the response is reliable, you can use the command on the ground or from the saddle during riding and schooling.

## Body Posture

The best seat in which to ride is undoubtedly the traditional classical seat, which can be modified, whilst retaining its major principles, for riding at the fast gaits and for jumping. It is best because it gives the rider superb balance in a 'minimalist' seat which does not confuse or agitate the horse. It allows clear aids to be given more easily than in 'busier' seats and does not create or permit 'white noise' caused by movements made by a rider trying to stay on or in balance. Fashions in seats come and go and different disciplines, such as different types of showing and different forms of jumping, develop their own seats, but underlying them all the classical seat continues on sublimely as an utterly reliable 'home base' to which to return when other seats let down you or your horse, or go out of style. You cannot go wrong with it.

## THE CLASSICAL SEAT

The classical seat is described in many good books on riding but a reminder of it is entirely appropriate for this book as it is truly a horse-friendly seat. So many riders are familiar with it yet do not adopt it fully although, as a teacher, I find that many people believe they do. Just like standing and walking with good bearing and posture, riding in the classical position requires a bit of effort in order to become second nature. It is easier to slop around or, at least, just not to put those finishing touches to it which give it all its advantages over other ways of riding.

Looking at a horse and rider from the side, the rider's head should be balanced straight on top of the neck with the face vertical. If it is tilted or held forwards or backwards or with the chin up or down in any way it will, believe it or not, affect the balance and function of the whole of the rider's body and, therefore, the horse himself.

An observer should be able to see that an imaginary, vertical line runs down from the rider's ear, through the shoulder, through the hip and elbow and on through the ankle joint. Some say that the line should run down the back of the heel but it is the ankle bone which does the flexing and the absorbing of the weight, not the heel, so it is the ankle joint which should be positioned beneath the hip joint at the bottom of the line for ultimately effortless balance.

There should be a straight line from the rider's elbow, through the hand, down the rein to the horse's mouth. This gives the most direct feeling in and of the horse's mouth and so allows the most sensitive touch.

From the front and the back, the rider's shoulders, elbows, hips, knees and feet should be level in their pairs. This is achieved by sitting equally on both seat bones in a well-balanced saddle. (The subject of the effects of tack and uneven muscular development in the horse is covered in the next chapter.)

It sounds simplistic to say that that's it, but, as far as the rider's position is concerned, it is. Keeping it and using it is where the practice and skill comes in and that is dealt with in the following sections. This position is applicable to halt, walk, sitting trot and also canter unless a 'light seat' is being used on a young or unfit horse or one with memories of back pain.

Other than for rising trot and jumping (see later this chapter), your upper body should normally be kept directly upwards with a straight torso, in tone and held there gently, but not stiff. Your shoulders should be pressed gently back and down: for a little more emphasis, try to feel as though you are sliding your shoulder-blades down into your back pockets. Do not, however, force anything. Just tell your body repeatedly what to do and hold it without creating stiffness. You should stretch your spine up from your waist. Feel that you are trying to touch the sky with the top of your head (you do not need to raise your chin for this!) and do not be tempted to hollow your back as you do it. So, you are actively *stretching* up from the waist and passively *dropping* down from the waist at the same time. Many riders find it helpful to push their seat bones forward very slightly – that is to say a touch, no more than an inclination, which helps counteract our natural tendency to stick our bottoms out too much.

Your upper arms should drop naturally straight down and be held there, again in tone but not stiff or rigid, with a down-and-back feel to keep your elbows on your hips. Most riders are not taught this and some ride with almost straight arms, which does nothing to encourage a sensitive contact on the reins and bit.

The base position for fast canter, galloping and jumping still accords with the classical principle of a balanced seat but the upper body is brought forward *from the hip joints, not the waist* so that the back remains flat, the shoulders are above the knees and the toes are below the knees. The lower legs are kept down and secure, the stirrup leathers remaining *vertical*. That is an important point for security and safety: if the lower legs are moved forward or backward from this position, the rider's balance and security and, therefore, control and safety are adversely affected. If the legs swing back, (a very common fault) the rider will be inclined to go too far forward and risk coming off over the horse's head or shoulders. If they swing forward the rider tends to either sit on the buttocks or brace against the horse's mouth (known as 'water-skiing'). This causes the horse, in turn, to brace himself against the hard contact and lack of balance, and his performance deteriorates from there.

The position described for fast work and jumping is variable within limits according to just what movement the horse is making. With shorter stirrups it gives you a secure, balanced seat which does not take you too far forward (which is dangerous) yet allows you to absorb more easily the movements of a faster-moving or jumping horse.

## USING YOUR SEAT AND POSITION

Many people underestimate the importance of the seat and the whole of the legs as aids, often using too much hand and only the lower legs, or even just the heels. The seat can be used not only to help you to stay on but also to ask the horse to go in a certain direction – forwards, round curves, laterally and to slow down or stop, or even to go backwards.

The main feature of the seat is that its usual or 'default' state is one of relaxed buttock muscles and a feeling of opening the seat and spreading it across the saddle. You must aim to sit upright *on your seat bones*, not back on your buttocks, where you will be out of balance. The correct, classical seat is more like *standing* around your horse than *sitting* on him and although you should aim for a deep, adhesive and therefore secure seat, this does not mean sitting heavily. Sitting heavily causes many horses to drop their backs or, at least, be understandably reluctant to raise them, and a dropped back is the opposite of what you want, as explained in Chapter 9.

Supple hip joints certainly help. To give you the feel of a 'full' seat whilst you are getting used to it, open your hips and completely relax your buttock, thigh and lower leg muscles so that you can let your legs drop, toes down, without stirrups, loosely around and down the horse's sides. It is ideal to do this on the lunge if you can find a friend or teacher to lunge you on a steady horse. The feeling is one of the seat and legs being draped around the horse like wet tea towels – in contact but not being pressed on.

In my experience, most pupils, when on the lunge or otherwise riding without stirrups, are taught to keep their toes up. The only way you can do this is to contract the muscles down the fronts of your lower legs, which inevitably stiffens them – not a good idea. With stirrups, the toes are up because the stirrups are on the balls of the feet and the weight is dropping down through the heels, not because the rider is using their leg muscles to keep them up. So, without stirrups, let your toes dangle down and, in the early days of learning this horse-friendly, relaxed seat, it does not matter if your legs swing around a little. Concentrate on sitting on your seat bones, upright (neither tilted forward on your fork nor leaning backward on your buttocks) and feeling the movements of your horse's back underneath your seat. You cannot feel these movements adequately if your buttock and thigh muscles are tense and contracted.

Once you have got the knack of staying relaxed but of sitting upright on your seat bones, dropping down from your waist and stretching up from your waist, and without hollowing your back, you will find that you can feel the rising and dipping of the horse's back under your seat and the swinging of his belly and ribcage from side to side, as he walks, and later trots, along. As his right hind rises and goes forward through the air, the right side of his back will dip and his belly and ribcage will swing to the left against your left calf, and vice versa. This sensation will enable you to tell which hind leg is moving through the air. The reason you need to know this is because *it is only when the leg is moving through the air that you can influence it by giving an aid*. If you aid the horse whilst the leg is on the ground he cannot comply at that instant, may become confused and give you the impression that he is not listening to you, or is slow or lazy.

Whilst doing this, be most careful to keep your upper body straight upright and your shoulders level, not least because a crooked, unbalanced rider certainly affects the horse's own balance and his movement. He has to cope with you as well as his own body, and as a top-heavy, influential load on his back, you can be quite a problem if you are out of balance, too busy or expecting him to work within restrictive and/or badly timed aids.

You have to learn to let your seat be moved passively by the horse at this point from *below the waist*. Think of your body as being in two parts – your upper body above the waist belongs to you and your lower body (seat and legs) belong to the horse. Concentrate on keeping your shoulders level but allowing the two sides of your seat, left and right, to dip and rise with the movements of your horse's back. It helps if you lean back very slightly. (Actually, this should perhaps be more a sensation than a fact. Most of us think we are upright when we are very slightly inclined forward, so the 'feeling' of being slightly back may actually represent being fully upright.) If you concentrate on relaxing and feeling your horse's movements, you will find that you are doing sitting trot with no problem.

To take back your stirrups, raise your *toes*, not your knees, and ask a friend on the ground to put your feet in the stirrups so that the balls of your feet (the widest parts) are on the stirrup treads. You may now need slightly longer stirrup leathers than formerly. Let the weight of your legs drop perpendicularly down to the ground through your heels. This will normally cause your heels to be naturally lower than your toes, if you also keep your ankles flexed.

Remember, do not think that it is good to sit heavily in the saddle because this equates with security. What it does is encourage the horse to drop his back, which is exactly what you do not want. Draping your seat and legs *around* your horse helps you to adhere softly to the saddle and gives your horse a secure feeling, too, of a reliable rider who is light to carry (known as 'riding light'), relaxed and blending with his movements but securely in control, with no stiffness or jarring in the seat. Horses transform when ridden in this way.

The stirrup leathers should be approximately of correct length when the stirrup treads touch your ankle bones when your legs are dropped without stirrups. If the leathers are too short, you will not be able to drape your legs around your horse sufficiently and you will lose some of the 'in contact' area of your body. You will also be inclined to sit back on your buttocks instead of up on your seat bones. If your stirrups are too long, though, you will be 'tip-toeing' around, maybe losing them and feeling for them, and your legs will be unstable and your security compromised. For flatwork, use the longest leathers you can which also give you comfort and security. For jumping, again find your comfort level, which is usually around three holes shorter than your flat length.

Ride around in this relaxed but controlled seat and start to develop a little 'tone' in your legs so that they stay in position without stiffness. It helps to think of telling your legs to just touch your horse's sides and of pointing towards your horse's hocks with your heels.

*In sitting trot*, with or without stirrups, as well as allowing your seat to be moved up and down by the movements of your horse's back, there is another movement which keeps your seat blending with your horse and this comes from the small of your back. In the suspension phase of trot, if your seat and thighs are properly relaxed you will not be thrust up out of the saddle (although some horses move their riders more than others) but you can improve your own and your horse's experience of this gait if you allow the small of your back to flatten in the suspension phase and hollow in the ground phase. In the suspension phase, feel as though you are almost sucking your horse up under you with your seat and thighs, and letting him gently down again as he lands. The alternate, very subtle flattening and hollowing of the small of your back easily permits this *if* you remain relaxed. Your hip joints also play a passive role by very slightly closing in the moment of suspension and opening when the horse is grounded. Remember to keep your movements gentle and minimal. By doing sitting trot in this way, you will feel really at one with your horse and he will be able to flow along using his body well instead of resisting a constant, rhythmic thumping on his back.

*In rising trot*, riders' legs often flap out on the 'rise' and in on the 'sit', which indicates that they are pushing up from the feet and not controlling their legs. One consequence of rising like this is that, by placing all your weight on to your stirrups this, in turn, is transferred via the leathers up to the stirrup bar/tree point area of the front of the saddle and, unavoidably, down on to your horse's back just behind and below the withers. Concentrate instead on keeping your legs close to your horse's sides without pressing them on and certainly not gripping. They won't do this on their own – you have to gently but definitely keep them there. Do this by taking some of your weight down the insides of your thighs and letting the rest drop down through your heels. This horse-friendly technique adds to your horse's comfort by relieving him of marked on-off pressure as you first rise (or rather swing forward) and then sit. A poorly performed rising trot can cause even the best-fitting saddle to rock slightly from front to back, with a constant change of pressure on the horse's back, which cannot be very comfortable for him.

In rising trot, the basic movement is not 'up and down' but 'forward and sit'. As mentioned, do not push yourself up with your legs from the stirrups but keep a *downward* feeling on them, with freely flexed ankles, and let the horse help you to move the lower part of your pelvis, your pubic bone and seat bones, forward, clearing the saddle just enough to make the movement possible. Then, as you sit again, *slightly* tuck your bottom underneath you, rather than letting it stick out behind you. This creates a minimal movement which is reassuring to your horse and keeps it all neat and balanced.

*In canter*, the main feature is to keep the relaxed but toned vertical seat, but to ride with your inside seat bone *and shoulder* (depending which leg your horse is on) slightly more forward than your outside ones. This applies whether you are on a straight line or a curve (rounding a corner or performing curved school figures such as circles, spirals or serpentines). If your horse is in left canter, for instance, move your left seat bone and shoulder slightly in front of your right ones. This is, again, comfortable and very reassuring to your horse because it fits with how his back works in canter. In left canter, the left side of his back is mainly in front of the right side, and vice versa.

It is common for riders to place the outside shoulder forward in canter and when doing curved figures, but this creates a twist in the body which the horse can detect, and it does put off many horses and make work more difficult for them. When the shoulders are kept above the hips there is no twist and the flow of the dynamic forces through the rider's body (and down to the seat) and the movement are natural. You cannot 'push' or nudge the horse around a curve with your outside shoulder as is so commonly taught. So, if you want to canter or turn right, you put the whole right side of your body forward *a little*, and if you want to canter or turn left, you put the whole left side of your body forward *a little*. This is logical and more comfortable for both horse and rider. It is not a large movement – there is no need to exaggerate it – but it makes a big difference to your ease of movement, your balance and to the sensation you give your horse.

The canter footfalls themselves explain this. The horse will start left canter with his right hind, land his left hind and right fore together, and finally land his left fore. His left feet land in front of his right feet throughout left canter and, of course, vice versa for right canter. If you keep your seat bones level with each other, you are not positioned 'with' him and he can feel this slight discomfort. (This is a common cause of horses having difficulty achieving correct strike-offs in canter, and of breaking gait from canter into trot.) Therefore, in canter, the position and action of your seat should be a slightly diagonal, rocking one; again, keep your seat relaxed and spread over your saddle, and the small of your back and hip joints supple so that you can actually move with your horse's movements.

*Do not rock backwards and forwards* in the canter. Keep your upper body upright and let all the movement happen below your waist.

Your legs support the above positioning. Your outside leg should be moved from the hip slightly back behind the girth ready to give the aid and, once in canter, to rest down the horse's side to help keep the quarters in line with the forehand. Your inside leg should rest downwards against his side 'on the girth' which, in practice, means fractionally behind it and a little further forward than the outside leg.

A big advantage of this combined positioning of legs and seat in canter is that it is a unique 'position aid' which confirms to the horse that you want him to canter on the appropriate lead and to stay in canter as long as you keep your seat bones positioned that way.

*To ask for a transition to canter*, in sitting trot or walk, place your inside seat bone and shoulder forward and your outside leg back a little, two or three strides before you are going to give the aid. This warns your horse that it is coming and so does not take him by surprise, which will worry some horses, so that they do not make a smooth transition, or may even 'run' into the wrong lead. Ideally, you should give the actual canter aid when the leg which starts the movement is just lifting, so as his outside hind is lifting (his back has just dipped to that side and his ribcage has swung towards your inside leg) give an inward on-off squeeze or tap with your outside leg, which is already back a little, and you have a good chance that he will oblige, particularly if you release the inside rein a little – which helps many horses.

*To ask for a transition from canter to trot*, all you have to do is to return your inside seat bone and shoulder and your outside leg to their positions level with their pairs and the horse will trot – there is no need for a hand aid or a slow/stop seat aid. This is another aid which horses seem to understand naturally and react to calmly.

Of course, when initially teaching any transitions or resolving a training problem, always use the vocal command for the gait you want.

*To slow or halt with the seat,* sit very upright, keep your seat relaxed but 'hug' your horse with your thighs, ceasing to move your seat and hands with his movements. This tells him that the current movement, gait or speed is no longer wanted. (You can combine this with a gentle on-off feel on your outside rein if the seat alone is not quite understood, but try without it first.)

*To ask for forward movement,* nudge your seat bones clearly forward a little. Some horses do not respond naturally to this, even on a loose rein, but it is a technique to which your leg aids can diminish in time; do not think that it is out of your orbit. It is not a particularly advanced technique and most horses who are in the habit of working *with* you soon catch on. It helps if you use your vocal commands to teach it. A horse used to this technique can be put into canter simply by means of a forward lift of the inside seat bone, and flying changes can be performed by simply alternating the forward lift of each seat bone during the moment of suspension in canter – right seat bone forward and up for right canter and vice versa. This is *so* much more refined and horse-friendly than kicking with spurred heels and tilting the body over sideways to the required side, collapsing at the waist and hip at the same time, all of which simply makes life, and compliance, more difficult and unpleasant for the horse.

## SEAT ADAPTATIONS FOR JUMPING

Today, in teaching, much emphasis is placed on training the rider not to get too far forward as this weakens the seat and is a situation in which falls are more likely to occur if the horse checks his speed, refuses or runs out. In most falls, riders fall over the horse's head or shoulders; rarely do they come off sideways or backwards.

The sensible aim is to ride in as balanced and secure a seat as possible and in a way which gives the horse complete freedom both to see his fence and to negotiate it, without the rider hampering his movement or interfering with his balancing pole – his head and neck. This all has to be done by the easiest means possible for full effectiveness.

Get into practice by riding at canter on the flat, with slightly shortened leathers, in a light seat, with your seat maintained just above the saddle. Since this can be tiring if you are not used to it, practise initially for very short periods, so that you do not find yourself bumping on the horse's back, or supporting yourself by the reins. Try to find some gently undulating ground on which to practise the technique and don't progress to jumping (especially significant obstacles) until your balance on the flat is confirmed – if you cannot yet maintain balance on the flat, you will not be able to make the postural adaptations necessary to stay 'with' the horse when jumping.

The following method of jumping makes it easier for the rider to adopt a still, balanced and secure seat without getting too far forward, and permits the horse full freedom to jump naturally with no interference from his partner.

Approach the fence on a light contact so that the horse can hold his head in a natural position to enable him to see it clearly. As he takes off, fold *down from your hip joints with your back flat,* push your seat *back* without letting your legs swing forward and push your hands *down* and *forwards* diagonally towards his mouth, keeping your straight line of elbow-hand-horse's mouth.

Another way of achieving the latter movement is to keep your hands and arms soft and think of the horse drawing your hands down and forwards towards his mouth with the lightest of contacts on his mouth. On the descent and landing, bring your upper body upright again but avoid banging your horse on the back as he regains his balance and gets away. Keeping your ankles flexed throughout the jump will absorb the considerable forces from your weight and will go a long way towards helping you stay secure.

This technique has been used most successfully by world-class riders for decades but is seen less often now, certainly not because it does not work or is 'outdated' (which good riding never is) but because it demands an independent, balanced seat and also hands which are independent of the body. These take a bit of time and trouble to develop (most effectively by doing grid work or jumping small fences on the lunge without reins) and I find that most people now do not want to take the time and/or make the effort.

What we often see today is a quite different seat and technique. In the approach, when the horse needs a very light contact in order to have the freedom of head and neck necessary for him to see the fence, we often see, conversely, a very firm contact resulting in the horse struggling for his head so that he can see clearly. At the moment of take-off, riders often pull back with their hands to help them lift their upper bodies up and forwards when they should be folding down as described above. They then often lean well forward, swing their lower legs back, push their hands up the horse's crest and, holding firmly on to the reins, lean on the horse's neck with their hands to help them balance. This effectively holds in the horse's head and stops him stretching out over the fence to (a) get over it and (b) use his natural balance in full stretch. On the landing and getaway, the rider, lacking balance, bangs back down into the saddle.

This is clearly far from a horse-friendly way to jump. It results in horses learning to adopt a lurching, stiff jump with a restricted head and neck which, in turn, forces them to use the wrong motion and muscles to get over the fence, with the high probability of suffering chronic injuries and developing an understandable dislike or fear of the whole process. Sadly, if the horse makes his objections known by 'misbehaving', rushing, running out, refusing or bucking and charging off on landing, harsh methods of 'correction' are used, which make him hate and fear his job even more.

## The Legs

Your legs can be used to brush, squeeze, tap or hug. A forward brush indicates that you want forward movement, a backward one (combined with a vocal aid, a lightened seat and a still, gentle but resisting bit contact – no pulling backwards, of course) tells the horse that you want rein-back.

If a light brush does not produce a response, you can give on-off squeezes with your calves or, if the response is still not there, taps. Be certain that you are not stopping your horse with too much bit contact, a stiff, hard seat or an anxious or cross attitude. Remember to use your voice to command the gait or quality you want. A tap (not a smack) with your whip behind your leg and/or, if you are wearing spurs, an on-off press with them should do the trick. Also, if your horse is not moving forward from your seat and leg aids, do not hesitate to take both legs back from the hip and squeeze or tap with them further back than normal. This stimulates the hind legs more and most horses will then produce more energy.

As soon as your horse responds as you wish, cease your aids so that he associates them with moving as you asked. This is his 'reward', which I have put in inverted commas because it is doubtful that horses understand reward as we do. You can praise him as soon as he moves by simply saying 'Good boy'

Provided you have good control of your various leg positions, blunt, rounded spurs can help you to make your point, if used tactfully, and to position your aids more precisely.

or whatever phrase you have chosen to let him know he has done the right thing, or stroke his withers with the backs of the fingers of your inside hand.

The gentle but present 'hugging' aid with your (dropped) legs, usually your thighs but sometimes your lower legs too, can be used to steady a fractious horse, to help him rebalance and to call him to attention when persistently distracted. Also, gently but reassuringly press your reins and hands in, keeping contact with both sides of the horse's neck or withers, again sort of 'hugging' him with the reins. This seems to give many horses more confidence, especially if you also use a calming vocal aid, such as 'Easy'. Depending on the horse, both aids, or one set, can be maintained for a few seconds, or given and released. Some sensitive or 'hot' horses find restriction unbearable or worrying, so a relaxed, spread seat with dropped legs and fingers which open and close can all be used to reassure the horse, to get his attention and ask him to try to concentrate. It is a case of seeing which works best for the horse you are riding.

*The position of your legs* also helps the horse to understand what you want, and their pressure in a particular place naturally encourages the horse to move that part of his body, like your hand moving him over in the stable, or a horse nipping him in the field.

Using one leg a little further forward than the normal riding position encourages the horse to move his forehand. Mostly, one leg will tap or squeeze in this position to move the forehand away from it. Using both legs in the normal riding position which, in practice, is just behind the girth, tells the horse that you wish him to move straight forward. Using only one leg there encourages him to 'bend' around it by moving his ribcage away from it: this aid is supported by laying the outside leg a little further back to prevent the hindquarters swinging out, and the inside rein also gently 'feels' to ask for inside flexion whilst the outside one is laid sideways on the neck to keep the forehand from moving outwards. If you put one leg back from the hip and use it well behind the girth, it asks the hindquarters to move away from it, and if you use both legs in this position it constitutes a more persuasive aid to stimulate the hind legs. However, don't force or overdo the latter, to the extent that you tip forward on to your fork.

## The Reins and Bit

*The outside rein* is often known as the master rein. It should mostly have a consistent but certainly not stiff or rigid contact. It controls speed mostly by passive resistance and a tightening of the fingers of your outside hand, and also indicates direction away from it, being used *sideways* just in front of the withers to turn the forehand. Just use intermittent pressure to send the forehand away from it, using as many little pushes or taps as you need to get your response. This is a powerful but gentle, old classical aid which horses seem to respond to naturally. In time, if you wish, all you will need to do is touch your horse's withers with a finger and he will turn.

*Your inside rein* is used for communication, to gently feel and release (by alternately squeezing and relaxing your fingers, *never* by pulling backwards) on the inside jaw, as required, to get the horse to give (flex) to the bit on that side. He does this correctly by flexing at the poll (not a few vertebrae back down the neck) and by slightly opening his mouth by flexing the joint just below his ear, which attaches his lower jaw to his skull. It is obvious that his noseband must be loose enough to allow him to do this.

The inside rein also helps in turns by being held lightly inwards and a little *forwards*. Pulling backwards on the inside rein, as is so commonly seen, causes a multitude of problems. For one thing, horses hate it; it only turns the head and neck, not the rest of the body (and does not even do that effectively, simply 'scrunching' the inside of the neck) and it often causes the nose to tilt in the direction of the desired turn without actually producing a good turn.

This inside-hand aid is an old, classical technique used to great effect to invite a horse into a curved track, whether a circle, a bend or a school figure. The thumb is simply turned, in this case right, into the bend with a very light contact or actually loose rein, and it works as if by magic. Pulling on the inside rein is a crude way to turn a horse: horses turn in a natural, balanced way when the aid pictured is used, especially when the rider also directs the horse by means of a slightly forward position of the inside seat bone and shoulder, or by stepping down a little into the inside stirrup.

The aid described in the preceding drawing, applied with both hands this time as a really effective and light way of stopping or significantly slowing a horse, in any gait. The rider should also 'hold' the horse with a still seat and thighs and bring the upper body *fractionally* back a little (without allowing the feet to swing forwards, of course).

All this spoils the horse's whole-body balance and co-ordination and it looks really crude to knowledgeable onlookers, because it is.

Used in conjunction with the seat aids described above, these two main rein aids – the pushing of the outside rein and the inviting, light, inward positioning of the inside rein (with a little vibration, if necessary) create balanced turns and a confident horse, who very naturally understands what you want and is willing to respond quickly and easily.

## HANDLING THE REINS

Your ultimate aim on a well-schooled, made horse should be to treat your reins as though they are made of silk, with a present but tactful contact on your horse's mouth (the subject of contact is dealt with in the next section).

*In a single-rein bridle*, it is usual to ride with the rein underneath your ring or fourth finger, the reason usually given being that this is your weakest and most sensitive finger. Most of the time, think of holding the part of the rein which comes up over your palm and out with a firm but light pressure between the pad of your thumb and the middle bone of your index finger. You can exert a quite strong enough 'grip' with this hold for most situations. It gives the rest of your hand freedom and independence and means that closing your middle two fingers around the rein will shorten it and increase the contact whereas opening them will lengthen it and lighten the contact, all without even moving your hand – let alone your wrist or arm. In this way, you can play your reins according to what message you want to give your horse, and give and take effortlessly – and minimally.

*In a double-rein, curb bridle* try running the bridoon rein between your middle and fourth fingers and the curb under your little finger. This means that the reins are well separated by two fingers and are easy to manipulate individually. Also, the bridoon rein corresponds to the position of the bridoon in the horse's mouth (the uppermost bit/rein) and the curb rein to the position of the curb bit in his mouth (the lower bit/rein), which is logical. This principle works for both double bridles and pelhams. Again, you hold the two reins, together, between your thumb and index finger. To manipulate the bridoon, you flex or open your middle and maybe fourth fingers, and to manipulate the curb you flex or open your little finger. Obviously, to manipulate them both you flex or open your middle, fourth and little fingers together. Many people using double bridles ride with the reins crossed and hold them with the bridoon under the little finger and the curb under the fourth finger. Personally, I dislike this method because the positioning is illogical and it is not so easy to work the reins individually.

*In a double-rein, gag bridle* you can use the same hold but remember that the purpose of the gag rein is to raise the head. Many people use gags of various kinds with only the gag rein attached so it could be in contact even when the horse's head is in a good position, which does not make for a happy mouth. The correct and most horse-friendly way to use a gag bit is to use a snaffle rein attached directly to the ring on the end of the mouthpiece as well as the gag rein on whichever part of the bit (depending on its design) it is meant for. In this way, the snaffle alone can be used and the gag only be brought into action when the horse gets his head too far down and in, and maybe bores on the bit. In this case, apply contact to the gag rein and, as an added encouragement if needed, raise your hands straight upwards, *not* backwards.

English or 'Cheltenham' gags are also known for their braking power on hard pullers and, although this may be a rather extreme technique to which to resort, there are times when, on certain horses, you might be eternally grateful that you had the gag! (Note that certain bits, called 'gags', e.g. American and Continental 'gags', are nothing of the sort.)

## CONTACT

The time-honoured phrase 'self-carriage on the weight of the rein' – the aim of all educated and 'thinking' riders – describes a state of being in which a ridden horse is using his body to best effect (in collection with his back up and his weight back) and with, apparently, little or no contact on the reins. In practice, even with swinging reins, there is always some contact because the weight of the reins themselves exerts a slight pressure or 'feel' on the horse's mouth. Also, simply putting a different bit in a horse's mouth, without exerting any pressure on it with your hands, can change the position and carriage of the horse's head just by the way the bit hangs in the mouth and possibly the slight poll pressure its weight exerts on the bridle headpiece.

The weight of contact to which a horse responds best has to be determined with each particular horse, but the lightest possible contact should, ultimately, always be our aim. There is much argument about contact and, in general, there often seems to me to be too much contact used. The weight of contact I find effective and acceptable to most horses, other than the very sensitive and the more advanced, classically-trained horses, who can go correctly on the weight of the rein, is what I call a comfortable, hand-holding contact – about the same as you would use to take a toddler across a road securely but without hurting or distressing him. This is also often described as the amount of hold you would use to keep a small bird in your hand without hurting or frightening it.

If a horse appears to need more contact than that, he usually needs re-schooling to respond better to the voice and to bit and rein pressures. This undesirable trait often occurs in horses who have been ridden crudely with hands and heels rather than seat and legs because this way of riding tends to put horses on the forehand and it also makes them resist the bit. It also occurs in horses with conformational faults which incline them to going on the forehand. Also, riders who do not school their horses to take their weight back a little and lighten their forehands, go in better balance and not lean on the bit, are asking for this fault to develop. A common misunderstanding is that of speed versus impulsion: they are not the same and too fast a speed for a horse's current state of balance and body control causes him to be unbalanced, to go, again, on the forehand and bore down on the bit.

The other side of the coin is horses who 'evade the bit' because they fear its action. This is often also the rider's (past or present) fault, not the horse's. Horses who deliberately go 'behind the bit' are clearly making their fears known and those who confirm themselves in this habit can be very difficult to deal with. Amazingly, many riders think that horses going overbent and behind the bit look good and purposely pull in their horses' heads to adopt this faulty and damaging posture. This matter is dealt with in Chapter 9.

As horse-friendly riders, we need to educate our horses, either from scratch or remedially, to go on a contact as light and comfortable as can be used to obtain the correct response and way of going, and to work to continue to create responses to light aids.

If a horse seems to have any mouth or bit problems, the first thing to do is to have the teeth and mouth fully checked and treated, if needed, by an equine dental technician or veterinary surgeon. This alone can put things right once any soreness has healed. It is fair either to use a bitless bridle, or not ride the horse, until this point is reached. (Because this area is so sensitive, after such problems, horses sometimes remember the discomfort and act as though it is still there for a while, so patience is needed.)

If you have a problem with a horse resisting the bit, pulling or leaning, and you are certain that his mouth is in good order, try different bits with the aid of an empathetic teacher to find one or two which he seems to find acceptable and comfortable, and which also give you control. In general, I am not in favour of 'bitting-up' horses into stronger and stronger bits, but do find that many horses who do not respect or like snaffle bits go very much more kindly in a pelham (see Chapter 6 Tack).

Horses with the opposite problem, that of going overbent or behind the bit to avoid its pressure, also – perhaps surprisingly to some – often go better in a pelham. Gag bits, properly used with a snaffle rein and a gag rein, which is only used when the horse tucks in his chin (often dropping his head at the same time), can help to get many such horses out of that habit. They soon come to associate 'tucking in' with the upward feel of the gag rein and greatly improve their way of going *provided* that the rider uses a sensitive contact when using both reins. There is no point in subsequently using a strong contact on the snaffle rein, as that will encourage horses like this to tuck in their chins, and you are on a self-defeating roundabout.

The best way of avoiding mouth or bitting problems is to do your best to develop sensitive hands which 'get through' to the horse but do not cause him discomfort or pain. This will involve developing an independent seat and the ability to use your hands independently both of your body and of each other.

Pulling back on the reins is very hard to resist sometimes, but is not the best way to use your aids. It is very true that 'it takes two to pull' – but what to do? It is much better to use passive resistance, which is rooted mainly in the posture and musculature of your lower back and abdomen, so that the horse is pulling against himself, with a strong-elastic type of feeling on the outside rein and a give-and-take with the fingers only on the inside one. Alternate the use of the reins to give an unpredictable feel in the mouth, as well. This, plus a bit that the horse respects but accepts and is not afraid of, is the best overall way of dealing with pullers. (Bolting, along with other potentially dangerous behaviours such as running backwards, serious napping, rearing, bad shying and spooking, is outside the scope of this particular book.)

Never saw your horse's mouth from side to side, but devise kinder, more effective ways of delivering an intermittent feel in his mouth which he cannot lean on or resist against. It is very effective to use your voice and your seat as described earlier to ask your horse to slow or halt, and, if you have the

*Above left:* When we received this picture from our photographers, they had captioned it simply 'Ouch!' and that was putting it mildly. This horse is clearly in a lot of pain and fear as can be seen from his head-carriage, the expression on his face and his frightened eyes. His tack indicates that he is used to being strapped 'up and down' to 'control' him as he naturally tries to avoid the habitually harsh techniques of his rider.

*Above right:* In contrast to the other picture, this horse is being ridden tactfully on a kind contact. Horse and rider are 'in touch' but the horse has enough freedom of his head and neck. He is going freely forward, happy, relaxed and interested in his surroundings.

space, to direct him into a gradually decreasing spiral in order to slow him down. He will have to do so because he will reach the point where he cannot balance at the speed at which he is currently travelling, or in his current state of balance (or rather lack of it). No horse wants to fall down.

## Combining Weight Aids with Other Aids

The seat can also be used for a very effective and natural aid to which horses respond quickly and easily, unless their riders prevent them by applying contrary aids. That aid is the use of weight through your seat. *Where you put your weight your horse will almost always go.*

As described earlier, it is perfectly possible and feasible to ride and direct your horse largely with your seat and leg aids. Weight is simply another dimension of the seat. The reason why horses respond naturally to weight aids is because they want to be comfortable and also safe: they do not want to lose their balance. Their instinct is to stay on their feet so if, for instance, they feel more weight on the left side of their backs because the rider is either placing more weight on the left seat bone or pressing down more into the left stirrup (which will transfer weight up to the saddle via the stirrup leather and bar), the horse will move left to even up the balance again.

He cannot know, of course, whether or not the rider means to do this. If the rider is crooked, out of balance or riding more on one side of the saddle than the other, or if the saddle is moving to one side or the other (maybe because of uneven muscular development of the horse's back or the way he moves) and taking the rider with it, the rider's weight will be unevenly distributed and the horse will move to the side on which he feels the most weight.

This weight principle is often described in our terms as imagining that you are carrying a fairly heavy backpack. If it moves to one side or the other, you will move or lean that way to get under the weight and then try to hitch the pack over to centralize its weight again.

A lot of things in riding do not come naturally to we humans. For instance, adopting the 'foetal position' and grabbing on to the reins when we are frightened is exactly the opposite of what we should be doing. An example involving weight is where a horse leans in on curved tracks such as corners or circles, usually with his head to the outside to help him to balance. This, also known as banking or motor-biking, is the horse's natural way of turning at speed and you can see it in horses playing when loose and free. The head and neck (his balancing pole) are normally turned to the outside as otherwise he could well lose his balance and fall. This posture also occurs under saddle if the horse is travelling too fast to carry the rider's weight on the curve on which he is travelling, for example on tight corners or small circles or bends, so slowing down will help avoid it. It may also happen if the rider leans (as many do) even slightly into a turn (for example, if the horse is cantering to the right, the rider leans right): this shift of weight unbalances the horse who resorts to his natural way of retaining balance – head and neck and often hindquarters to the left and body angled to the right. This is uncomfortable to sit on and, if the rider continues to lean right 'with' the horse, this just makes matters worse. The way of riding a curve under saddle that is often recommended (i.e. when a horse needs to adapt his 'natural' movement to accommodate the rider's weight and requirements) is for the rider to keep sitting upright and to keep asking the horse for inside 'bend' and flexion (in the example given, to the right). In this way, the horse can retain his balance. If the turn still feels difficult for the horse, the things to do are slow down and (especially with a young or stiff horse) keep to turns that are based on larger circles.

This 'dressage' method of riding a curved track is certainly more aesthetically pleasing and more comfortable and controlled than motor-biking. In some sports, particularly Western barrel racing, where speed is of the essence, the horse's natural way of turning at high speed is used but, even then, most riders keep their upper body upright as the horse turns to help keep the pair of them on their feet – or rather, the horse's feet.

To best way to *prevent* banking is to prepare properly for your turn or circle and have the horse correctly flexed before going into it. If the horse is very green and not yet capable of this, restrict yourself to large circles at the slower gaits and generally ride corners shallow. Going deep into corners (even in walk) on a very green, weak horse, means that you are asking him to perform part of a very small circle, which is a quite advanced movement.

Preparation is, in fact, a key aspect of riding any turn, corner or circle correctly. *To direct your horse on to a curve,* look forward around the curve and bring your inside seat bone *with your shoulder immediately above it* forward a little, controlling the hindquarters with your outside leg back a little from the hip. The rein aids are an open inside rein (in and forward a little), and outside rein laid on the neck. You can also, with great effect, tap lightly on the outer side of the withers with your outside knuckles, or even just one finger. To the horse, this means 'move away' and he will move to his inside. Remember to open the outside fingers a little to permit this.

*Once you are on the curve*, in walk and trot your seat bones should be parallel with each other along the radius of the circle with your shoulders immediately above them. In canter, of course, the inside seat bone and shoulder should be a little in advance of the outside ones, as described earlier.

*To come off the curve*, simply look ahead to where you want to go and position yourself accordingly, and the horse will change direction smoothly.

If, despite your best preparatory efforts, you do find yourself on a horse who *is* banking, slow down, sit *upright* and put more weight on to your outside seat bone, also stepping down into your outside stirrup, with flexed ankle and a deep heel. This action and your position and weight transfer is a large part of the corrective process. You can also ask for more 'bend' around your inside leg and flexion of the horse's head and neck by squeezing firmly inward with that leg, also asking for inside flexion by feeling (*not pulling*) on the inside rein. Remember to 'allow' with your outside rein, which should also be pressed against the outside of the horse's neck to complement the inside rein aid.

Correct (logical) placement of your weight also helps in lateral work. Slightly weight and bring forward the seat bone (with the shoulder on the same side directly above it) on the side towards which you want the horse to travel. You can also place a little weight down into your stirrup on that side to emphasize the aid. Do not tilt or lean that way; just stretch your leg down close to his side and he will feel the required effect. Using your weight in these ways will make the movement so much easier for him to understand and perform, provided your other aids are correct. So, in leg-yield to the right, for instance, slightly weight your right seat bone, and your right stirrup as well if you want more emphasis, and give an intermittent squeezing or tapping aid with your left leg, or simply intermittent pushes to the right with your left thigh and knee, depending on what your horse responds to best. Ideally, give the aid when (in this example) the left hind is lifting.

## MENTAL/VISUAL COMMUNICATION

A lot of people scoff at the idea that you can 'think' your aids to your horse, but I know from years of experience that it can be a great help. I have used this method consistently and, yes, I am certain that I can do it, if I wish, without using any physical aids, depending on how tuned in I am to the horse, and how much the horse is concentrating on me. I believe that this is one of the main ways in which horses communicate with each other, too – which may be why it can work between human and horse.

All you have to do is to picture, imagine, to your horse what you want to do. At first, do this whilst you are giving your normal aids and, as your horse gets used to your doing it, you should be able to diminish your aids and try just 'thinking' to him. You can do it on the ground as well as from the saddle. Just give it a try and plenty of time. You do need a very calm, focused state of mind for it to work.

I remember an acquaintance of mine years ago who could go to the paddock and, even if the horses were not aware of him, just look at and 'think' to any horse there, and mentally visualize the horse turning and walking towards him, and it always worked for him.

*Looking where you are going* is also a good idea! Many, many riders look down at their horses' heads most of the time. If you look ahead, for instance, around a circle for about a quarter of its distance, it does help you to negotiate it correctly and your horse will move more freely and confidently. If you want to aim for a certain landmark, such as a tree or an arena marker, just look at it and position yourself to go there and it will happen smoothly and brightly.

## Breathing as an Aid

I was interested to read in Jenny Rolfe's book *Ride From The Heart* (see Further Reading) about the breathing techniques she has developed to help her communicate with her horses. I have used breathing in time with my horse both on the ground and in the saddle for years to establish 'one-ness' with horses, but find that Jenny's methods add another dimension to this. Very basically, a deep, outward sigh stimulates horses into action and a sharp intake of breath helps to slow or stop them. It is well worth a try, as is anything which helps to make your aids lighter, more minimal and clearer to your horse.

# ARTIFICIAL AIDS

## Whips

Whips, in horse-friendly riding, are used as an extension of the rider's leg to reach parts the latter cannot reach and to assist understanding, or to support a leg aid if the horse, knowing what it means, does not respond brightly enough. They can also be used, of course, as fly-whisks and it is noticeable how horses who are habitually well treated know the difference between these uses. I believe that whips should never be used to hurt a horse and, in order to give an accurate idea of just what level of application is meaningful but not painful as a correction, I always suggest that riders first hit themselves with the whip as hard as they intend hitting the horse, should the occasion ever arise. (Few will do this!)

You can use a long schooling whip for working on the flat, or a more convenient, shorter whip for jumping, which will not catch on jump stands, trees or hedges. Depending on the nature of the horse, some will go much more 'willingly' (note the inverted commas) if the rider just carries a whip and many will respond to a whip simply being waved instead of making contact, or to a rider hitting their boot rather than the horse. Horses react to whips in various ways, from being terrified or angry if you simply carry one, to taking little notice of even a firm smack with one.

The different feels or touches with the whip are significant to the horse. Very many horses these days are frightened of whips (many more than in previous decades, I find) and, with patience, some but not all can be trained to realize that their current rider/handler is not going to hurt them with a whip. Start by just stroking the horse's shoulder with the hand part of the whip, then his lower neck and chest, then along his back, trunk and hindquarters and down his legs – maybe over a period of weeks – whilst a friend is feeding him his favourite titbits, to get him used to the idea that whips are now associated with good things. Horses often seem to become more frightened of whips the further back on the body they are used, so this is worth remembering.

With a schooling whip, you can use it in a stroking manner or by just laying it against the horse to ask him not to move to the side where it is, or by tapping with it to ask him to actually move away from it, to lift a leg, or to use his leg more energetically. It should be borne in mind that you cannot use a whip whilst you are holding a rein without some feeling being transferred down that rein to the horse's mouth. This can be really confusing to a horse and it is better by far to let go of the rein before using the whip – although most people do not do so.

Some trainers can be seen riding with a whip in each hand. This is not because they are whip-happy but to relieve themselves of the need to keep changing a single whip from hand to hand.

Jumping whips are used behind the leg to back up leg aids or down the shoulder as reminders to concentrate or put in more effort.

## Spurs

Even completely blunt, rounded-end spurs should not be used by riders who do not have excellent control of their legs and feet. Many people think they have this ability but do not have it in practice, and consequently can inadvertently abuse their horses.

Spurs are meant to enable the rider to give a more precise, refined aid than is possible with the calf or heel of a boot. Some horses, it has to be said, do not co-operate as well if their rider does not wear spurs and, in these cases, they are used only as firmly as needed to get a response, as a back-up should the leg aid be treated with disdain.

Some riders claim that only spurs with rowels (filed blunt) should be used because these can be rolled on the skin which, they claim, is kinder than a potentially bruising prod with a blunt spur. This may well be true but you can still cut the skin with blunt rowels if you lack the necessary finesse and leg control.

Many spurs have flat ends with the edges smoothed off and these look acceptable to many people, but in practice they, too, can easily tear or cut the skin.

Roller-ball spurs have a smooth, synthetic ball fitted into the end of the spur which almost completely does away with drag on the skin and so are very kind but just as effective as ordinary blunt spurs.

## TIMING, REWARD AND CORRECTION

Because horses learn by the association of ideas, linking an action with a result or effect, it is crucial to get your timing right when aiding and rewarding or praising your horse. If you give an aid and the horse responds, you must stop giving the aid immediately so that the horse will link the action he has just performed to the aid that stimulated it. This alone is sufficient to establish the aid and action in the horse's mind, but most horses appreciate praise as well. To let your horse know you are pleased with what he has just done, you should reward him with a stroke on the withers or your chosen praise word or phrase within one second. Leave it two, or certainly three, it is claimed, and he will not link the praise with the act you want to reward.

This also works with correction. This can be a point of debate with those trainers who believe that you should praise the good things a horse does but ignore the bad things. I absolutely do not agree with this approach. Horses need limits, boundaries, parameters – call them what you will. Their natural way of functioning amongst their herd members involves learning what is acceptable behaviour, and what is not. If they did not learn correct equine social behaviour they would be regularly injured, and in the wild this can compromise their survival. Horses apply these 'manners' to humans, too, and feel calmer and more secure when we apply them to them, as they understand this way of interacting and know where they stand.

Correction is not punishment or abuse. You can correct a horse with a quietly spoken 'No', provided he understands it. This has been covered in the earlier section of this chapter on using the voice. It is mentioned here to emphasize that the same rules apply to correction as to praise and reward.

Correction *must* accompany the unwanted behaviour so that the horse links the act with the correction. This absolute accuracy of timing is essential, otherwise the horse will become confused. For instance, if the correction is too late, the horse may link it to whatever he did immediately *after* the unwanted act – which may be something of which the rider approved. So, in terms of the horse's understanding, he was 'corrected' for something he did right. This business of correction is a big responsibility for the rider, who must also be absolutely certain that the unwanted act was not performed because of rider error such as seeming, to the horse, to have asked for something of which he was incapable. *If you are in any doubt at all about such a matter, it is safer not to correct the horse, but simply continue as though nothing had happened.* Generally, if a horse does something on the ground or under saddle which you do not want, and you are *sure* this was avoidable on his part, a sternly spoken 'No' or a tap with the whip (a firm tap is usually sufficient) is enough to let the horse know that what he did is not acceptable, but it *must* accompany the misdemeanour so that the horse links the act with the correction.

If a horse, in a group of others, nips one of them he may well get an instant kick from his victim unless the latter is a shrinking violet who prefers to simply vacate the immediate vicinity! Usually, retribution is instant and we must mimic this timing system if we are to be understood.

However, so often we see riders really whipping horses who have done something they did not want, and leaving it several seconds before doing so. This is plain and simple abuse, not correction. Also, it does not achieve the rider's aim of letting the horse know he has misbehaved because the rider has left it far too long for the horse's mind to make the connection.

Learning, practising and using the techniques described in this chapter creates the foundation which underpins a rider's natural talent and flair and, without which, full potential will not be realized. Natural ability plus sound technique is a formidable combination, but even if you feel that you have little natural talent, working on learning and using correct and proven techniques which are humane (and many of which horses understand naturally), will still enable you to become an effective, educated rider. However, no matter what books you read or teachers you have, only *you* can make yourself put these techniques into practice.

# CHAPTER 6

# TACK

The importance of comfortable, well-fitting and humanely-adjusted tack, which is also suitable for the horse for whom it is intended, is one of the most under-rated aspects of horse management and riding. The whole business of choosing the right equipment for your horse can be really confusing because of the overwhelming range of tack and related gear now available. It seems that every week or month a new product or a new design for a familiar product is launched on to the market, which leaves us feeling that we've got to have it and that, if we do, our horse will be suddenly transformed into the horse from heaven. However, it seems to me that 'keep it simple' is generally the best advice here. The phrase, 'all the gear and no idea' is increasingly applicable to many sports nowadays, riding included.

Some products, new and old, do fulfil their promise and turn out to be really helpful, but others do not. Also, many people buy a product which sounds good in the advertising and magazine write-ups but is totally useless or even damaging in practice.

Of course, there is the ever-present, unavoidable fact that, even in ideally designed tack which is perfectly fitted and humanely adjusted, the horse can still be extremely uncomfortable and distressed if the tack is not used properly, or he is badly ridden. *Even if you have not tacked up a horse yourself, you have an ethical responsibility to check that the horse is comfortable and not subject to undue restriction, pressure or to discomfort.* Doing so may also be in your own interest, in case something fitting badly changes the horse's behaviour, or some item is actually defective.

*Since this book is not specifically for beginners, you may be surprised to see the following section on fitting and adjusting tack. The reason it is here is because I find that very many people rush the job and do it quite roughly, which must be pretty unpleasant for the horse. Also, many seem to have little idea of how uncomfortable and stressful tack can be to a horse when it fits badly and is adjusted wrongly.*

Consideration for the horse should always be paramount when choosing and applying tack or any other equipment. Simply put yourself in his position and imagine how you would feel. Do the job politely, confidently and gently. If he objects there is always a reason, so try to find out why: it may be a memory from past clumsy treatment, maybe even years ago, but you can get over this by treating him properly, talking to him and giving him treats during the process so that he associates it with enjoyment.

The first principle to understand when choosing and fitting tack is that it must be comfortable. Discomfort and pain are completely counterproductive to horse-friendly riding and to good results. When a horse's simple mind is concentrating on his discomfort or pain and on how to avoid them (which some riders take as misbehaviour), he cannot put his mind to what we are trying to teach him or get him to do. Even if the message gets through, the work required will not be well performed and the horse will probably make the association between work, and maybe that movement specifically, and discomfort or pain. Therefore, every effort must be made to ensure that all a horse's tack is comfortable.

His other equipment, too, such as boots, rugs, headcollars, training aids and so on must fall into the same category, because constantly battling against or putting up with discomfort and pain are exhausting both mentally and physically, as many of us know. You cannot take too much trouble over this issue.

All leather needs to be kept well cleaned and softened, from the newest to the oldest. Good, proprietary leather dressings are available which help with this and it is good practice to dress (oil) the leather occasionally, especially if it is not going to be, or has not been, used for some time. However, there is also a lot to be said for cleaning with glycerine saddle soap after every use or two, and when the leather has become wet from sweat or rain. Hard, dirty leather is uncomfortable and causes sores even when well fitted.

# SADDLES

Saddle fitting is now a recognized art and science and qualified saddle fitters are increasing in number. In the UK, professional qualifications in saddle fitting are awarded to those who have passed courses organized by the Society of Master

Saddlers. (It should be noted that a saddle fitter is not necessarily a saddler, and vice versa.) Some people are trained by a particular company to work with a range of saddles specific to them: others will fit a wide range of saddles from any manufacturer and may be freelance or employed by a particular tack retailer.

## Basic Rules of Fitting

The basic rules of saddle fitting still apply:

This saddle is designed for jumping and faster gaits, with its moderately forward-cut flaps and knee rolls. It is fitted far enough back not to interfere with the action of the shoulders despite its cut but, correctly, does not press on the loins. The correct positioning ensures that the girth can lie well back from the elbows and will not be pulled uncomfortably into the backs of them, inhibiting the action of the forelegs. The stirrup bars are fitted forward a little to allow the rider to comfortably adopt a balanced, fairly forward seat for cantering, galloping and jumping.

- *In length,* the saddle must be long enough, and also have a large enough under-seat panel, to spread the rider's weight evenly over as large an area as possible on the horse's back to reduce concentrated pressure on a small area. The saddle must also be made in a shape which mirrors the shape of that particular horse's back. Horses vary widely in conformation but most well-conformed horses have a smoothly undulating back, dipping a little from the withers and rising at the loins to the croup.

  Saddles which have a flat profile to the panel often cause 'bridging' – a common fault today – exerting too much pressure in front and behind but not making enough contact in the middle. This is sometimes a result of the flat shape of the under-seat panel and sometimes down to the fashion for deeply gusseted panels under the cantle area. This feature is aimed at stabilizing the saddle on the horse's back but many such designs create uncomfortable or even painful pressure under the cantle if they do not align with the shape of the horse's back and his musculature.

  The saddle must not interfere with the action of the shoulders in front and must not press on the loins at the back, a general guide being that it should not extend past the horse's last rib.

- *In width,* the saddle must sit down around the horse's back and be wide enough to settle comfortably (rather than be perched on his back) but not so wide that it rocks and bruises the sides of the withers. Also, it must not be so narrow that it pinches the withers and/or the muscles behind the shoulder-blades.

- *A good general guide* to width and whether or not the saddle 'bridges' is that you should be able to pass the flat of your fingers all around and under the edges of the saddle when the horse's heaviest rider is mounted, and under the under-seat part of the panel *evenly* to check whether or not it is bridging. The old guide of being able to fit the width of three fingers between pommel and withers when the heaviest rider leans forward in the saddle still has some merit although, if the saddle passes this test this *by itself* does not necessarily mean that it fits well in other respects. Also, note that purpose-built close-contact saddles tend to be lower than this in front, but they should be tested to ensure that the pommel does not press down on the withers when the rider is in a more forward seat than used for flatwork. All saddles must clear the spine along the gullet: check by looking down the gullet when the horse's heaviest rider is mounted.

- *In design and balance,* unless the saddle is intended for specialist showjumping, with forward-cut panels to allow for markedly shortened stirrup leathers and a consequent forward knee position, the lowest part of the seat should be in the centre of the saddle, where the rider's seat bones go. In a specific jumping saddle, for either cross-country or showjumping, the stirrup bars are often set forward to allow for a cross-country/jumping seat, and such a positioning is no good for correct flatwork. This positioning will constantly pull forward the feet and legs of someone riding at flat length, tipping them on to their buttocks and making the maintenance of a correct, balanced seat for flatwork a constant problem, or even an impossibility.

## Types and Designs

Many disciplines and even breeds of horses have saddles made especially for them. There have long been flat and very straight-cut show saddles with also a cut-back head or pommel, to appear as inconspicuous as possible on the horse's back and to show off his front. Their seats are often designed specifically to place the rider further back to give the appearance of the horse having a 'good' (long) front. Such saddles are less in favour now, many riders opting for better balanced ones which permit a correspondingly better balanced seat, not to mention comfort for the judge.

Saddles which are used for Working Hunter showing (in the UK) and general- or all-purpose saddles meant to cater for general jumping and flatwork are slightly forward cut. Dressage saddles come in many designs intended to put the rider in the traditional classical position. The VSD (a German abbreviation conveniently rendered into English as Very Slightly Dressage) designs are a very useful compromise between pure dressage saddles and those for general flatwork or very small jumps.

With regard to saddles for body shapes, rather than specific disciplines, there are saddles for low-withered native ponies and cobs (who are often rather barrel-shaped and hard to keep a saddle on) and breed-oriented ones such as for Arabians, and they all come in various widths and lengths, so, with a bit of searching, you should be able to find a suitable one which is comfortable for both your horse and yourself. It has to be said that high-withered horses can be a problem, and many appear so because they have been fitted with saddles which are too narrow for them and which have, through excessive pressure on the muscle tissue just below and behind the withers, caused hollowing in the horse's back there. Such horses also tend to show reluctance or inability to work correctly because of the memory of or association with the constant discomfort experienced under saddle. A cast-iron test of this problem is to walk such horses down a steep hill and carefully note their action. A lot of them will creep down sideways to try to avoid the pressure of an already tight saddle pressing in behind the shoulder-blades. However, once such horses are fitted with a wide enough saddle (and following correct remedial schooling), they can come right and be brought round to correct use of their bodies, the test being that they can easily walk straight and freely down the hill – given that there are no other problems, that is.

Saddles adjustable in various ways, either to accommodate changes in a horse's shape, or for use on different horses, have been available for some time and innovations continue in this field.

*Adjustable gullet or adjustable head/pommel* saddles, which can be narrowed or widened to some extent can work well. However, with some of these, a degree of expertise is either essential or helpful to ensure that the adjustments are carried out properly. Also, some people report that, in certain designs, widening of the pommel may result in the gullet to the rear being narrowed, so it is as well to question a supplier closely on this matter.

*Flexible tree* saddles are available which, carefully fitted to avoid rubbing as the tree moves with the horse, can be extremely comfortable for the horse. *Treeless* or *half-tree* saddles are also available, all aimed at increasing the horse's comfort and enjoyment of his work. However, some people have experienced a tendency for such saddles to slip on certain shapes of horse, so caution is recommended if you wish to explore this option.

*Floating panel* saddles have separate panels attached under the seat by means of shock absorbers. There is more than one type and many people, and horses, like them but, as with any saddle, they must be carefully fitted by someone trained in their use and function. Within limits, the shock absorbers allow the saddles to be readjusted and used on any horses with similar conformation, although this is not a five-minute job. The one I bought for an old Thoroughbred mare who had muscle atrophy behind the withers transformed her working life.

*Air-filled panel* saddles are aimed at preventing uneven pressure on the horse's back as, of course, air moves with the movements of the back. As with many saddles, one hears good and bad reports of them but they are very well worth investigating.

*Exchangeable block* saddles have knee and thigh rolls which can be changed or adjusted according to the rider's needs as far as fit, comfort and discipline are concerned. If investigating these, remember that, while it is important that the saddle helps the rider's position, this should not involve actually 'wedging' the rider in place and taking away some flexibility of position.

## Numnahs and Pads

Most people use numnahs, pads or saddle cloths now although many saddlers maintain that they are unnecessary if the saddle fits correctly. The fact that leather is absorbent means that a numnah for sweat-absorption is redundant but, still, many people feel that they add to their horses' comfort.

The main point to remember is that they must do exactly that. If they cause any uneven pressure or friction under the saddle they will create problems, not comfort. Saddle pads or numnahs with sewn or bonded seams round their edges must be big enough for those edges to come outside the

An important but often overlooked point is that the numnah or saddle pad must be pulled fully up into the saddle gullet so that it is not pressed down on to the withers or spine by the saddle when bearing the weight of the rider.

edges of the saddle. Those made of hard foam materials need to have finely chamfered edges if they are not to form ridges under the saddle, and pads and risers must conform to the same criteria. Remember, also, that anything put underneath a saddle will affect its fit, usually adversely. An originally well-fitting or tight/too narrow saddle will feel tighter, but a too-wide one may feel more stable. Using anything intentionally to adjust the fit of a saddle is only a temporary measure: the saddle itself should have attention as soon as possible.

## Girths

A girth should keep the saddle on and in place without being fastened too tightly, and should be smooth and comfortable with enough 'give' in it to allow the horse to breathe properly, although some interference with breathing will be inevitable. With a horse who does not carry a saddle well or easily, finding and fitting the right girth can be quite tricky.

Because the girth goes round the horse's ribcage, which houses the lungs, I feel it is essential for it to lengthen and shorten with the expansion and contraction of the lungs and ribcage, because it must be awful to have to work actively yet be unable to take deep breaths and breathe properly. Elastic inserts at *both* ends or in the centre allow this. Those with elastic at one end only cause the saddle to be pulled over to the side which has no 'give' when the horse breathes in, and then back again when he breathes out. This is no good for his comfort as it must feel awkward and create uneven movement, pressure and friction.

Some fabrics are claimed to have a flexible quality in them and, therefore, throughout the whole girth. I find that the flexibility in these is so minimal as to make no significant improvement to the horse's comfort. Some, also, have crossed fastenings which are claimed to move with the horse, but I have not found that these make a significant difference to comfort or the confidence of the horse to breathe freely, which is crucial to humane treatment.

The design of girth which is cut back away from the elbows is excellent for comfort and free movement of the forelegs, and there are several types available now. Just make sure that the cut-back part is, indeed, level with your horse's elbows. Short dressage or belly girths have a lot to answer for in this department as, in many cases, the buckles come at just this spot.

A lot depends on the horse's conformation, of course, but girths in general cause a lot of discomfort to horses, I am sure, and should receive as much care in their selection, fitting and adjustment as the saddle itself.

## Stirrups

Uncomfortable stirrups can cause aches and pains in your ankles, 'pins and needles' and general difficulty in sitting comfortably and riding well. There are many designs now which flex and give according to your foot and leg position and movements, and have absorptive treads built in. Those with wider treads than usual can be very comfortable, especially if you ride for long periods and, all in all, the advances in stirrup design are very much to the benefit of rider and horse.

## Thoughts on Saddling

*It is also now the fashion to put on saddles much too far forward, which can cause several problems. The correct positioning of the saddle is behind the shoulders and withers (so that you can fit the edge of your hand between the top of the shoulder-blade and the front edge of the saddle) and in front of the loins: the saddle must obviously be a suitable length to permit this correct positioning. Many saddles are put on so that they actually cause weight-bearing on the back part of the shoulders and the sides of the withers. It may be that people think they will be in better balance if they can sit just behind the withers but, in practice, things do not work that way. The problems caused by putting on a saddle too far forward are:*

1. It unbalances the saddle which (in most designs), is intended to place the rider's seat bones in the centre of the seat. In this positioning, the front is tipped up and the cantle is tipped down.

2. This causes interference with the movement of the tops of the shoulder-blades, which extend right up near the sides of the withers. The shoulder-blades rotate around a point about a third of the way down their length, so their tops go back when the horse extends his foreleg and the lower part goes forwards. This not only causes pressure at every stride on the tops of the shoulder-blades but also rocks the saddle slightly from side to side at the same time.

3. The back of the saddle is tilted back and can press into the back muscles under the cantle, encouraging the horse to hollow his back, trail his hind legs, hold his head and neck up in the air and, quite often, to buck and kick out in understandable objection. Even if the head and neck are forced down and in, the back remains hollowed.

4. The fact that the saddle is tilted up in front and down behind means that the rider is constantly forced to the back of the saddle on to the buttocks, with the consequential fault of feet and legs being pulled forwards. The ideal placement of seat bones in the centre of the saddle seat with (given correctly positioned stirrup bars), vertical stirrup leathers, is destroyed and so is the rider's balance, effectiveness and comfort.

5. When the saddle is in this position, the girth unavoidably lies too far forward, near the horse's elbows. Every time the horse's foreleg moves backwards, the girth digs in to him behind the elbow, so he experiences the very off-putting and uncomfortable effects of:
   - Pressure on the tops of his shoulder-blades with possible bruising.
   - Pressure on the back muscles near the loins, which is intensified by the rider's constantly sliding back towards the cantle.
   - Pressure behind his elbows.

No wonder so many horses tacked-up in this way do not work anything like as well or enjoyably as they could. Depending on his temperament, a horse may either put up with this unhappily or 'play up'. These effects apply to saddles for any discipline which are put on well forward.

A less common mistake than putting on the saddle too far forward is to put it on too far back. The main objections to this are that the rider is then seated too far back and so is out of balance, and this can mean pressure actually on the loins.

A design feature of some saddles which I personally dislike is point straps from the area of the tree point to the girth. Their objective is to keep the saddle stable but they are often done up too tightly (because they need to be to fulfil their intended purpose in this very mobile area of the horse) and greatly restrict the horse's movement and his breathing. I have always found that horses are more comfortable and work better if point straps are removed or absent in the first place. This brings us on to the topic of girthing up.

The first point I'd like to make on this topic is that very many horses resent having their girths fastened and very many owners get annoyed with them and do the job much too quickly and suddenly, making matters worse. The girth should be long enough for you to fasten on the bottom hole of the straps on each side without hauling it up, gradually tightening it one hole at a time in between putting on other tack.

Notwithstanding the need to girth up gently and gradually, the girth must obviously be tight enough to keep the saddle in place when you mount. As a guide to this desired level of tightness, you should be able to slide the flat of your fingers between the girth and the horse's side, but not pull it away. The desire to over-tighten the girth before mounting will be decreased, and the horse's comfort thus increased, if you can vault on or mount from a block or other convenient object. If you can do this without having to put one foot in the stirrup first, this will minimize any chance of pulling the saddle sideways. Remember to check the girth from the saddle when you have been riding for about 10 minutes, when it will probably need tightening a hole. Before you dismount, loosen it a hole so that, when your weight is off, it will not feel, to the horse, as though it has suddenly been tightened.

## BRIDLES

The purpose of a bridle is simply to give the rider control of the horse's head and, where appropriate, to keep a bit in the horse's mouth. Nosebands, which are not strictly part of the bridle (neither are the reins), have a very significant effect on the action of the bridle and bit. Again, the ruling principle is that the horse's headgear must be comfortable if he is to be able to concentrate on his work and be more inclined to co-operate. This does not mean that the bridle cannot be adjusted to emphasize certain points to the horse, such as adjusting the height of the bit or the tightness of the noseband, but never to the extent that the horse is uncomfortable, or caused pain or distress.

The tendency today in many quarters is to have bits too high, sometimes very high, and nosebands too tight – often far too tight. So-called 'crank' nosebands, which have been available for some years, are designed so that the noseband round the horse's upper and lower jaws can be fastened so tightly that the horse has no hope of opening his mouth and, therefore, reacting correctly to the bit. In turn, the fashion for tight bridles and nosebands has brought on to the market various designs of padded headpieces and nosebands advertised as 'humane' because they relieve the pressure when all that is needed is for the equipment to be adjusted correctly and comfortably in the first place.

## Basic Points of Fitting a Bridle

The first golden rule is that your bridle needs to pass the 'finger test' if it is to be horse-friendly. You need to be able to slide a finger *easily* under *every* part of your bridle and noseband to ensure that there is no unreasonable pressure anywhere. When asked to do this, many people avoid the headpiece and the noseband, possibly because they know that they are going to be too tight to permit it. The telling points on the noseband are the bridge of the horse's nose and under the lower jaw/chin groove area. If the headpiece is too tight, the bit is almost certainly too high. Try this finger test, and if you cannot do it, simply loosen the appropriate parts of the bridle until you can.

The remaining criteria are that:

- The headpiece must not press or cut into the backs or round the base of the horse's ears so, to avoid this, ensure that it is not too wide, especially if the horse's poll conformation seems to encourage it.
- Another reason why it might do this is that the browband is too short, a common fault on modern bridles. It simply needs to be the right length to lie straight across the horse's forehead, neither pulling the headpiece forward nor flopping up and down as the horse moves.

A well-fitting snaffle bridle worn by a Fell or Fell-type pony. The browband is long enough to lie snugly but not tightly and to prevent the headpiece being pulled into the back of the ears (a common cause of head-tossing). The throatlatch is long enough to prevent the pony feeling uncomfortable about flexing at the poll (by its contact with the throat). The noseband looks comfortably loose and far enough below the facial bones not to rub them. The bit is a comfortable height in the mouth, creating one wrinkle at the corners of the lips.

This horse is wearing a bridle designed for the show ring, with narrow leather to show off his head. However, the browband is too short and is pulling the headpiece into the back of his ears and the throatlatch is far too tight – and he is showing his discomfort by the unhappy expression on his face. This type of noseband (front strap only) is used for neatness. The bit seems to be a comfortable height.

- The throatlatch should be loose enough to permit the full width of your hand between it and the round jawbone, so that it drops halfway down it. If it is too short, even if it does not actually press into the throat, the horse will sense it and be discouraged from flexing to the bit, either at the poll or from the jaw joints just below the ears.

- The cheekpieces should not come so far forward as to rub the corners of the horse's eyes – again, often the result of a too-short browband.

- The noseband must not rub any part of the head, the most common part being the sharp facial bones. It must be loose enough for the horse to be able to open his mouth slightly, in other words flex his jaw so that he can gently mouth and accept the bit rather than having it forced on him with his mouth clamped shut.

# BITS

The choice of bits has always been overwhelming and now it is even more so than before. There are several complete bitting 'systems' on the market, as well as our extensive collection of traditional designs plus rare bits, new individual designs and the weird and not so wonderful. Again, your guideline should be comfort for the horse, combined with sufficient respect for the bit to give you reasonable control. I say 'reasonable' control because riding is always a risk sport and no horse is 100 per cent controllable.

It is said that the hands on the other ends of the reins are more important than the bit itself and this is certainly generally true, but it also has to be admitted that some horses give poor, unwanted or inadequate responses to some bits and it is a case of trying different ones until you can meet the criteria given in the preceding paragraph, for both your sakes. You will know whether or not you have control – but how can you tell whether or not your horse is comfortable? The answer is simply by his behaviour when ridden and by his facial expression which a knowledgeable, empathetic person on the ground will have to tell you about.

To make an accurate judgement about the effectiveness and comfort of bitting, you have to be absolutely certain that it is not your hands which are causing the problem by applying too firm a contact (dealt with earlier), by pulling back, by being over-active (jiggling about or sawing) – in short by not being trustworthy and mainly still. Also, you have to be certain that your seat is independent enough to ensure that you do not brace yourself against the horse's mouth or use the reins/bit to keep yourself in balance (or even in the saddle).

If the horse is too 'busy' in his mouth, champing the bit rather than gently mouthing it; if he is producing excessive froth and saliva; if he tosses his head; if he fights or resists the bit; if he thrashes his tail; if he goes with his head tilted or twisted; if he rears or offers to do so, or does anything other than appear to be happy and confident, it is a good pointer to a problem with the bit (or, of course, a dental or mouth problem).

Regarding the tell-tale facial expression which, unfortunately, the rider cannot see from the saddle, your observer should look for a tight, tense look about the face, head and maybe neck. The ears may be back (perhaps laid flat back if the horse is angry), the eyes may be wide and alarmed or half shut and

This horse has been so cruelly ridden that his mouth is actually bleeding. His tight muzzle with protruding top lip clearly show his pain. His tight bridle and martingale and the obviously very strong bit contact (a curb bit used, incorrectly, with a Grakle noseband) all add to the horrific scenario.

giving a 'closed-down' impression. The muzzle may be very mobile, with too much froth around the mouth, the lips may be drawn back, and the nostrils wrinkled up and back.

There are some widely held ideas about bits which need addressing.

1.  The first is that *a thick mouthpiece is kinder or milder than a narrower one.* Modern research has shown that the tongue of almost any horse takes up far more room in the mouth than was previously thought. Many horses, in my experience, actually prefer and go better with a mouthpiece which is fairly slim. It was thought that a thick mouthpiece spread the pressure more in the horse's mouth and that a thinner one intensified it but, of course, the amount of pressure applied depends on the rider's hands.

2.  *Flavoured bits encourage a soft mouth.* How do we know that a horse actually likes the flavour of the bit we have chosen for him, or the feel of the material from which the bit is made? I feel it best to err on the safe side and use tasteless materials and to give a horse his favourite titbit (most horses like mints) just before putting the bit in. This encourages a relaxed jaw and mouth and the taste will stay with him for quite some time. I understand that some materials from which bits are made actually cause a mild irritation, which is what causes the saliva to flow and makes some people think that the horse's mouth is being made soft. I would not want this effect on my horse.

3.  *A simple snaffle is best.* First, what do we mean by a simple snaffle – a half-moon/mullen-mouthed snaffle, a straight-bar snaffle or a single-jointed snaffle? A half-moon snaffle can be comfortable for some horses as it allows room for the tongue, but a straight-bar snaffle must be really uncomfortable as it does not. A single-jointed snaffle also does not conform well to the lie of the tongue in the mouth and can poke into

the roof of the mouth. Jointed snaffles with a lozenge or link in the middle, creating a double-jointed mouthpiece which is moveable and conforms to the tongue, are more comfortable, provided the link does not press into the tongue.

4. *Curb bits are cruel.* It is much kinder to use a light pressure on a curb bit with a correctly adjusted chain rather than a heavy pressure on a snaffle. I nearly always find that horses are very happy and settled in a mullen mouthed/half-moon pelham bit. Double bridles, with their two bits (a thin snaffle or bridoon and a curb bit) are too much of a mouthful for many horses. Although they are regarded by truly competent riders as the bitting arrangement *par excellence* (as they are said to allow such riders greater finesse in applying aids), sadly, many doubles are used by people who are far from competent – but so are pelhams. *Any bit is cruel if it is roughly or clumsily handled.*

5. *Bits should be fitted high, creating several wrinkles, to keep them steady in the mouth and increase sensitivity.* This is one of the unkindest of modern ideas. Stretching the skin at the corners of the lips like this causes pain, splitting of the skin and even permanent callouses – hardly humane or likely to encourage a light mouth. Also, the bit is constantly giving the horse a 'stop' or 'slow' aid because of its pressure, which will discourage many horses from going freely forward. It also makes the bit more difficult for the rider to manipulate with any finesse. All this is counterproductive to good, humane riding.

## The Correct Fitting of Bits

There are clear standards for fitting and adjusting bits which have been used reliably for generations. The position of horses' teeth makes these standards suitable for most horses unless the horse's teeth are unusually positioned. If in doubt, ask your vet for an opinion.

- *Unjointed snaffles, Kimblewicks and pelhams* (and similar bits) should comfortably touch the corners of the mouth without causing any wrinkles.
- *Jointed snaffles* should create only one wrinkle at the corner of the mouth.
- *The bridoon of a double bridle* should be fitted in the same way as a jointed snaffle.

Checking that the bit is a comfortable width for the horse's mouth. You should be able to fit the width of one finger between the horse's cheek and the bit ring.

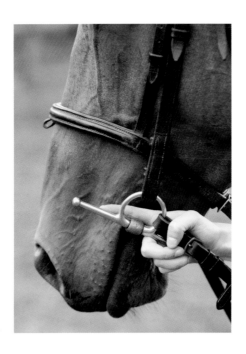

- *The curb of a double bridle* should NOT touch the corners of the mouth but should lie under the bridoon in the mouth and hang about half an inch (1.2 cm) below it.

Regarding *width*, you should be able to fit the width of an average-sized finger between the corner of the lips and the cheek or ring of the bit, on one side. If a bit is too narrow it will pinch and be uncomfortable but if too wide it will slide from side to side and may bruise the mouth.

## Bitless Bridles

There are now quite a few different designs of bitless bridle. Some are very simple side-pull bridles which involve a direct 'feel' on the rein on either end of the noseband, some rely on tightening round the lower part of the head (the upper and lower jaws) in various designs, some use pressure on more parts of the head and the strongest types operate on leverage from cheekpieces of varying lengths, the tops of which are attached to a noseband and with the reins fastened to the bottoms of the cheekpieces. The latter designs can be very strong if used harshly.

Bitless bridles in general are good for horses with apparently insoluble mouth problems, but some horses are just happier in them and this, of course, is fine provided you also have adequate control. Unfortunately, the argument that the more comfortable and the happier the horse is, the more likely he will be to co-operate with his rider by no means always holds true. Some just take complete advantage and leave the rider feeling helpless, but (another argument again) this may be because the horse's initial training and his responses to vocal commands have not been sufficiently confirmed and established in the horse's mind to make obedience a habit with him.

Whatever your viewpoint or your reason for using a bitless bridle, there is no doubt that they can be very successful for some combinations, who have performed tremendous feats using them. The same principles of comfort and fit apply as for ordinary bridles.

# TRAINING AIDS

The only two training aids I have ever felt like using are the Chambon and the de Gogue.

The Chambon (pronounced *shombon*) has long been very successful in showing a horse the most comfortable and advantageous place to hold his head and neck in the earlier stages of schooling, or for the remedial schooling of those who have developed a high-headed carriage with, consequently, a dropped back and disengaged hind legs and quarters. It is mainly for use when schooling from the ground – lungeing, long-reining or leading in hand as part of a remedial programme. It creates pressure to poll and bit when the horse raises his head too high, which is released when he lowers them.

An argument against the Chambon is that it does not influence the hindquarters to engage. In fact, it does do so indirectly in the best way possible, by leaving it to the horse. When the horse's head and neck are in a good posture, the back will rise a little anyway, and this encourages the pelvic tilt or tuck which brings the hind legs further under the body.

The de Gogue (pronounced *de Gog*) serves the same purpose as the Chambon and has similar effects, but it can be adjusted for use either in groundwork (when the trainer, having fitted it, does not manipulate it during work) or on a ridden horse.

Draw-reins and running reins are often badly used, producing a forced, overbent head and neck carriage. With both items, if they are used very minimally by a sensitive rider and only when the horse's head rises above an advantageous position (often with a poked nose), a gentle feeling on the rein to the rider's hand can remedy this. To be fair and correct, it is essential that this be released the moment the head is lowered, otherwise the horse learns nothing except to go in an ugly, forced way with his head and neck well overbent and his chin tucked in. This posture can cause pain and distress and can injure the tissues of the head and neck, which no horse-friendly rider wants for their horse.

There are now many other patented devices, many of which operate on the hindquarters as well as the head. These, like any other device, can be misused by those who lack knowledge or are misguided – a category that

What a sad sight! This appalling and inhumane way of riding is unfortunately very common today owing to a complete misunderstanding about beneficial posture, muscle development and visual function in horses. The horse is badly overbent and restricted and almost certainly in a good deal of discomfort and possibly pain (and, therefore, mental distress as well) in his head, neck, shoulders and possibly elsewhere as he tries to compensate for the constriction of his natural balancing pole and his windpipe in the throat area.

includes some trainers. The main problem is that they are often adjusted too tightly and produce an artificial, damaging, hunched and 'squashed' posture and way of going. If adjusted so that the horse is encouraged to go in a correct outline with the front of the face in front of the vertical, and so that their effects are not felt when he goes correctly, they may have a place in schooling as a temporary measure to give the horse the idea of how to go. Otherwise, they can cause the effects described in the previous paragraph and, when they are removed, horses often *deteriorate* in their way of going and become quite confused.

When horses are coerced into a particular posture, or even made to hold what we regard as a correct one for too long (in my view, the acceptable time is only a very few minutes – certainly single figures and dependent on the horse's stage of fitness or development), they start to feel tension, discomfort and anxiety which can escalate into pain and fear. In such a state, they can only concentrate on relief and survival and not on what we are trying to teach them. Training, or rather abusing, a horse in this way is unacceptable on ethical grounds. Unfortunately, many people are not aware of the true effects of what they are doing and, especially when 'told' to do so by an instructor, believe that it is the correct thing to do. Understandably, it may never occur to them that their horse may actually be distressed and in pain.

This horse is being lunged in comfortably long side-reins which allow him to carry himself, correctly, with his nose just in front of the vertical. It should be remembered that unless side-reins are very long they inevitably force the horse to overbend if he is asked to lower his head and neck, so they should not be used at this length if asking the horse to go 'long-and-low'. They should be undone after a very few circuits, the horse encouraged to stretch his head and neck, and then fastened again, if required, for further work.

The practice of standing horses in their stables for long periods, strapped into an 'outline', mentioned earlier in this book, also comes under this heading.

When using any equipment on your horse, I hope very much that you will put yourself in your horse's place and do your very best to imagine how you would feel if you were in his skin and being schooled in that tack. Think really hard about what you are doing to him, or what your trainer may be doing or recommending, and study your horse closely for his subtle, or maybe not so subtle, responses. Decide whether or not you, in his situation, would feel physically comfortable and mentally secure and in the mood for learning and co-operating, or be suffering discomfort or pain, anxiety and fear, and desperately trying to work out how to escape.

It can be very difficult to intercede when an instructor or trainer is persuasively trying to get you to do something you feel could be wrong, or is riding or handling your horse in a way which concerns you, but your horse only has you to rely on to keep him safe. Other people are very unlikely to intervene, so it is up to you to do it. Most horses like working if they understand what is wanted and can physically comply. This can only happen if they are physically comfortable and, therefore, safe.

# CHAPTER 7

# Groundwork

Groundwork means, fairly obviously, working the horse from the ground rather than the saddle, and there are many versions of it these days. Over the past decade or two, the biggest change in groundwork has been the spread of so-called 'natural horsemanship' methods, mainly of Western but also Australian origin, which emphasize groundwork both in starting off horses (backing and riding away) and for remedial purposes when horses have developed behavioural problem (from our viewpoint) as a result of previous bad handling and riding. There are quite a lot of different methods of natural horsemanship and entire books, DVDs, videos and magazines are devoted to them.

Our traditional methods of European groundwork are lungeing and long-reining. Lungeing, in particular, is still more common than either long-

One of the most beneficial things you can do with a horse is to walk him smartly on a loose rope with complete freedom of his head and neck, encouraging him to carry them low (with the poll no higher than the withers and, ideally, lower). This causes natural stretching of his entire top line, brings up his back and promotes free and healthy use of his muscles.

reining or any natural horsemanship method. Loose schooling is also used, not only to get horses used to vocal commands and a trainer's body-position aids but also to exercise horses and often to introduce them to or bring them on for jumping without the encumbrance of a moderate or poor rider.

This chapter concentrates on lungeing, long-reining and loose schooling, and mentions my own favourite method of what I like to call complementary horsemanship – the Tellington Touch Equine Awareness Method – because it can be used alone or alongside traditional techniques and, in my experience, is supremely horse-friendly and very effective for both youngsters and spoiled horses.

## GROUNDWORK AS AN AID TO RIDING

Groundwork, done properly and thoroughly, is a great help in schooling a horse and instilling a good measure of understanding and obedience before ridden work starts. Along with correct handling, it brings the following benefits to the horse's education and development.

- He will, or should, have developed the habit of obeying all the basic vocal commands, which means that you have fairly good control over him, young though he is.
- He will be used to a headcollar, lungeing cavesson, bridle, bit, roller, saddle, boots, lungeing and long-reins and whips, and to being handled, groomed, having his feet picked up and being tended by the farrier and vet.
- He will understand being led in hand, having to wait at gates, not barging in or out of stables, not barging people in fields and so on.
- He will, through long-reining and, a little later, lungeing, have acquired a measure of self-balance and agility whilst under the control and direction of people, which will have started to build up his body and added to his mental self-control.

If you get these preliminaries right, being ridden is just a smooth progression in the things you do with him and, when he is mounted, he will already be used to a saddle, bridle and boots and will quickly associate correctly given aids with their vocal equivalents. You're already halfway towards working him independently of the lunge or an assistant.

# LONG-REINING

I am dealing with long-reining first as this can be started with well-mannered 2-year-olds in walk as a way to get them thinking and taking them around the place, preferably with a helper also leading, under better control than is possible when just leading them in hand. I do not approve of lungeing horses of this age other than in walk and feel that there is little to be gained by it because of the tendency of most trainers to use constant circles. On long-reins, horses can be taken on mainly straight lines around their home area, and learn about bends, without the stress of circles. In an arena, circles can be done, of course, but long-reining allows much more work to be done on straight lines, gentle curves (parts of circles) and shallow loops and serpentines.

I have always found that horses seem to enjoy long-reining and find it interesting, whereas many do not seem to enjoy lungeing. A lot does depend on the trainer, but it is not hard to understand this difference. Even though the horse may be listening for commands and learning to use his body in different ways, going round and round on ceaseless circles cannot be very inspiring for the horse and a circle is an unnatural and potentially physically stressful pattern. (In their natural state, horses very rarely move in complete circles.)

I am assuming that, before starting long-reining, the horse is readily obeying vocal commands and touches from hands and whip to guide him. He should also be leading obediently from either side. There are several methods of long-reining, but the one I describe is fairly simple for everyone.

## Equipment for Long-reining
You will need:

- A pair of long-reins or a couple of lungeing reins.
- A good lungeing cavesson and/or a bridle and bit.
- A saddle with stirrups, which should be down (to run the reins through) and tied together underneath the horse's breastbone to stop them swinging around. Alternatively: a driving roller with terrets to run the reins through, or an ordinary roller with dees on its saddle for the same purpose.
- Leg protection such as boots all round (I like combined brushing-cum-tendon boots). A finishing touch for safety is well-fitting overreach or

Long-reining seems to be insufficiently used today. This horse is going comfortably and well, although the author would like to see him extending his nose a little more beyond the vertical.

bell boots all round in case the horse treads on himself, either hind to fore or sideways. Some people also like to use knee pads.

- A long whip. I find a buggy whip, a groundwork whip or a polo or schooling whip more convenient than a lungeing whip with its thong and lash – although the last can still be useful.
- A long lead rope or half-length lungeing rein for your assistant.
- You and your assistant should wear hard hats, gloves and strong footwear.

*Side-reins* are a point for discussion and decision. I am not in favour of them for young horses as there should be no need for the extra control they give if the horse is properly schooled to the voice and touch and you have a competent helper. Later, when he is used to basic lungeing and you want to start to get him used to the feel of a bit of contact on his bit, they can be introduced. Of course, if you have a mature horse who is difficult to handle, you can get more control provided restraint does not actually frighten him. With any horse who is tricky or dangerous to handle, expert help should be sought.

If you do use side-reins, fasten them to the horse's natural, standing length of neck and head, then shorten them one hole only to give him an initial feeling of contact. Remember, later, that the horse cannot reach long-and-low, or have a stretch, in side-reins because they will force him to overbend as his head lowers – which is not only useless but also damaging. Some people both long-rein and lunge in a Chambon to good effect.

Needless to say, the horse must be accustomed to all this gear before being asked to learn long-reining. In the stable, have someone competent, firm and calm holding him whilst you gently but confidently touch him with the lines, first on his shoulder then, gradually, all over – especially his sides, hind legs and the backs of his thighs. By all means, finish there for one day, and don't actually take him out.

Put on the cavesson, maybe over a bridle minus noseband and reins if you (and the horse) are experienced enough to long-rein from the bit. (You wouldn't do this, initially, with a real youngster.) The cheekpieces of the bridle are brought out over the cavesson noseband before being fastened to the bit rings. The long-reins can be clipped to the side rings of the cavesson or to the bit rings, as appropriate. Get your assistant to hold them and the horse whilst you fit the roller or saddle. The roller goes in the same place as the saddle – behind the tops of the shoulder-blades and a hand's width back from the elbows – for comfort and security.

If you are using a riding saddle, drop the stirrups down and adjust them so that there will be a straight line from your horse's mouth, through the stirrups to your hands. Tie the stirrups together under the horse's breastbone with binder twine to stop them swinging about. If using a roller, pass the reins through the lowest dees for a novice horse or higher ones for a more experienced one. Your assistant should clip the lead rope to the front ring of the cavesson.

## Basic Long-reining Procedure

Take up your position behind the horse and ask your assistant to lead him out whilst you give the familiar command to 'Walk on'. Make sure your route is clear, familiar to him and secure, with no dogs or other animals, including horses, loose and able to get to your horse. Perhaps for the first day, just walk him around the yard, let him stop and look at things, walk him round on the other rein, and then take him back. On another day, you can take him into the schooling area and progress from there.

Do not start off in, or go too early into, a large, open field, particularly one he is used to playing in, as this is inviting lack of concentration and the anticipation of high jinks. Also, if he does manage to break away you could have the devil of a job catching him again and a lot of psychological harm, and maybe physical injury, will have been done.

Initially, you can hold the reins a little away from his sides, and gradually, purposely touch his sides with them. Do not irritate him with them, as this is asking for trouble: however, if he is well brought up and has felt the reins in the stable he should not be concerned. Eventually, you can move from behind him slightly to one side and back. You, not your assistant, should be giving the vocal aids. Do not be tempted to lean back on the reins which will, of course, create a sustained pressure on his nose or mouth. Treat the long-reins as though you are riding, and really emphasize your vocal aids.

You can perform shallow curves, regular halts (no hauling on the reins; just use your voice, a gentle, normal rein aid and, perhaps, a light pressure on the horse's chest from your helper), moving off again (remember to release the reins a little), large serpentines, S-bends and so on. Halts and immobility teach obedience and patience, and regular transitions start to work the rear end. If you can find some gentle slopes to walk him up and down, so much the better. Eventually, you can walk him over single poles.

Keep the sessions very short for a youngster; praise him every time he does something good, correcting with 'No' (and *never* a jab on the reins) when he misunderstands or lets something more interesting override your aids. Take him back to his stable calmly; if he is keen to get back there, check him with subtle aids as described above.

The whip is used to aid him, to help him understand what you want. The reins can help to keep the hindquarters straight, as can a touch with the whip. To get forward movement if he is unsure, just touch his hindquarters combined with a 'Walk on', and tell your assistant to look straight ahead and just go. You must both be calm, firm and positive, and not ask for too much too soon. This is just an extension of his daily life.

You will soon realize that you have to be fit and agile for long-reining, especially when you start trotting. Take things slowly and progress one step at a time. Don't trot until he is quite calm about all this work in walk.

It is quite true that you can take a horse up to high school level on long-reins. The UK's doyenne of this work is Miss Sylvia Stanier, LVO, whose books I recommend and which are listed in Further Reading. Long-reining at this level is an art in itself and can only benefit your ridden work, if you want to go that far.

## LUNGEING

Many people do not long-rein until a horse is experienced in lungeing, but if you start a youngster off on long-reins, with an assistant, lungeing will come to him much easier, as a 3-year-old or older.

Lungeing in this way, on large circles, in good balance and a natural 'long-and-low' posture has the same benefits as those detailed in the photograph on page 130, with the added advantage of encouraging bend and being able to work easily at gaits faster than a walk.

## *Equipment for Lungeing*

You will need similar equipment to that for long-reining:

- A lungeing rein.
- A good lungeing cavesson and/or a bridle and bit (the former, when first starting a novice horse).
- A saddle with stirrups, or a driving roller with terrets, or an ordinary roller with dees. (Not essential in the first instance, but for later.)
- Leg protection.
- A lungeing whip with thong and lash, or a buggy whip with no thong. (Preferably the former for the early stages.)
- A long lead rope or half-length lungeing rein for your assistant.
- Side-reins, if you choose them.

As with long-reining, accustom your horse to the equipment in his stable if he is not already familiar with it. Unless he has been abused with a lungeing whip, he will probably not object to it at all, but show it to him just the same to make sure, and stroke him all over with it, taking care that the thong is carefully wound up and held.

Before you go near a horse with a lungeing whip, practise with it to make sure you can run out the thong and accurately *touch* anything you want with it with a light pressure. Of course, the object is never to hurt your horse. If you know anyone willing to let you practise on them, take advantage of the opportunity!

## Basic Lungeing Procedure

With your assistant, take the horse to a safe, secure schooling area with good footing. Regard the earliest sessions as an extension of leading in hand. You will not need your whip at first. Your helper should stand by in case needed. Lead your horse round and walk normally, looking ahead. As you gradually get further and further away from him, he will almost certainly try to come with you. At this point, your assistant can walk by his head, using the lead rope only if necessary, to keep him out on the circle as you adopt a position facing his body rather than facing ahead. (A point to consider is that, if a horse has a good relationship with his handler, and is used to being led normally, it is entirely naturally that he should expect to stay close in the first instance. Therefore, initial 'turning in' is not a *disobedience*. People who are over-enthusiastic about trying to 'chase' the horse out on to a circle are simply causing confusion.) *You* give all the commands as it is easier for the horse to follow one familiar voice. If your horse is uncertain, your assistant can aid him manually.

When the horse is getting the hang of this, you can start holding the whip: if the horse is on the right rein, hold the lungeing rein in your right hand and the whip in your left, and vice versa. If, from previous work, there is evidence that the horse is currently one-sided, it is sensible to start him out on his 'easy' rein, simply because it will be easier for him at the outset. Obviously, the 'difficult' rein has to be worked on later. At first let the whip point behind you with its end on the ground, then slowly bring it into its normal position.

The positions of your body and whip constitute body language and direction to the horse. For normal forward movement, your body should face the horse's ribcage so that you form the top of a triangle; your rein hand forming one side of it, your arm with the whip the other side and the horse the base. If you point the whip at his hocks and stand level with his quarters yourself, slightly angled towards his head, this will encourage the horse to move forward, or do so with more energy and speed. Pointing the whip at his head or in front of him, with your body level with his head and angled towards his hip has a blocking effect and should slow or stop him. Horses become very adept at watching the whip position and obeying it, so do be careful only to move it when you mean to.

If you do not get the response you require and you are certain that you are doing everything correctly, run out the thong of the whip to touch the horse on the thigh for more forward energy, on his middle to keep him out or his shoulder to slow him. Snaking the thong horizontally behind him (not touching his legs) can encourage him to go forward and doing it vertically well in front of his head will stop him if he just wants to go on. (This is an action that needs some precision on the part of the person lungeing.) If you really have trouble stopping him, either he was not sufficiently confirmed in obeying your commands in hand or, at some point, he has been made to go round and round far too fast, which is very damging. This is a problem with many horses. Go back to in-hand training to get calmness, reliable obedience to the voice and touch aids, and progress slowly from there again. (It is a fact that many people are quite appallingly bad at lungeing and create all sorts of problems in the horse. If you have inherited such problems, you may have a lot of remedial work to do. Note that, if a horse has previously been chased out on to a circle, he may be quite dangerous to set off, and you may need to work on this aspect whilst being careful for your own safety.)

It is essential to use your vocal commands so that the horse knows what is wanted. As he catches on (which he should do fairly quickly if he has previously been handled properly), the assistant can gradually be dispensed with – but not until the horse will readily stand, walk on, trot and maybe rein-back. At this point, the horse should stay out on the circle, or return there if you point the whip at his ribs, so the helper will just be walking with him but not actually leading him. (To teach your horse to rein-back on the lunge, he needs first to be familiar with the command 'Back' and a touch on his chest during general handling in and out of the stable. Have him in a calm halt and ask him to back as you would in hand. He should back but if he does not do so, ask your assistant to pat him on the chest as you say 'Back', ceasing the instant he does so. If you have no helper, tap him on the chest with your lunge whip as you say 'Back', again, ceasing the tapping absolutely as soon as he backs.)

The object of lungeing is to start developing a correct way of going, and building up the right muscles, before ridden work starts, with its burden of your extra weight. *Every time your horse goes incorrectly he is developing the wrong muscles* so correct him when this happens. (This is explained further in Chapter 9.) At first, a neutral posture is fine to get him relating the commands to lunge work but, when he is reliable at this, you can introduce carefully adjusted side-reins or a Chambon to start encouraging correct work. However, while these devices (correctly adjusted and employed) can certainly help, it is often forgotten that judicious use of lunge line and whip (the equivalent of 'riding between leg and hand') can greatly improve the horse's way of going, without any supplementary equipment.

However, remember that correct, gymnastic work will probably be quite tiring for him and, for muscular health and to retain a happy, willing outlook, the horse needs to relax and walk with a completely long and free neck and head, to rest his muscles and allow the blood to flow freely through his relaxed tissues, in order to supply oxygen and nutrients and remove the waste products produced when muscles work. Just standing still with his head and neck free is also good practice.

The alternative – keeping horses in 'outline' for more than a short time – does damage, not good, as toxic waste products build up in working (contracting) muscles, causing fatigue and pain. At first, you may only obtain good posture for a *very* brief period, but praise your horse when he gives it to you, and he will gradually be able to work like this for longer, and will offer to do so. Eventually, after several weeks, depending on the horse's age, fitness and constitution, several large circles and other figures such as ovals or straight lines (with you walking with him) can be achieved in good posture and with the horse's hindquarters and legs engaged. As with a human working out or practising a dance or gymnastic routine, good work for a very few minutes interspersed with rest achieves more good than keeping at it without stopping and loosening up again.

*Never, ever ask or allow your horse to career round on the end of the lunge line, especially on too-small a circle, in a bad posture, as this is doing nothing but harm.* Many people allow their horses to have a buck and a kick on the lunge before starting work, but if the horse has not warmed up first this can cause injury by suddenly working 'cold' tissues, and it can be dangerous for the lunger. If a horse *does* initially 'explode' on the lunge, it is better not to try to stop this violently, because it can cause further problems, but he should be dissuaded and calmed down as soon as possible. As standard practice, I think allowing/encouraging this initial 'buck and a kick' is a thoroughly bad idea

Circles are more stressful than many people realize particularly when, as often happens, a thoughtless trainer sends the horse on or allows him to go too fast, out of balance, or will not let out the rein so the horse is on much too small a circle (which can actually be frightening at speed) and makes the whole process fraught with stress and anxiety. This practice can cause injuries to the limbs and body and is no way to bring on an equine athlete who, it is hoped, has a long working life ahead of him.

On the other hand, correct lunge work and, of course, good long-reining practice, are a tremendous help to the development of a riding horse, and make the rider-trainer's job much easier because of the developed habit of obeying vocal commands, the muscular development and the habit of watching and paying attention to the trainer.

## TELLINGTON TOUCH EQUINE AWARENESS METHOD (TTEAM)

This method is a complete system of bodywork, groundwork and ridden work and it is well worth studying the whole method, perhaps starting with Sarah Fisher's Book *Know Your Horse Inside Out* (see Further Reading). From the perspective of groundwork, the way of lungeing it encompasses is a little different from the traditional one.

A long lead is used, which has a soft rope or a chain on the end, fastened around the headcollar. The trainer holds the rein and a white 'wand' (like a white schooling whip) in the hand nearer the horse and walks, jogs or runs around with him accordingly. The white wand is easy for the horse to see and the method is more versatile than conventional lungeing as you can easily perform different shapes with it. When you want to change rein, you do have to change over the attachment to the headcollar, but this is little trouble.

There are two useful items of TTEAM equipment which could broadly be described as training aids and which can be used in hand, during long-reining or when lungeing in either this method or the traditional one. These are the body rope and the body wrap.

*The body rope* is a rope put over the horse in a figure-of-eight. One loop goes over the horse's head and the other goes round his hindquarters, lying under his tail in the same place as a fillet string, with the crossover point just

Part of the equipment used in the Tellington Touch Equine Awareness Method of groundwork and riding. This is the TTEAM 'body rope' used on a ridden horse, which has the effect on reluctant or uncertain horses of encouraging them to move forward more enthusiastically.

This is a ridden version of the 'body wrap' which is made up of an ordinary stretch bandage. It is passed behind the thighs and fastened to the girth straps under the saddle flaps. It has the effect of calming a horse at the same time as bringing him more 'together'.

behind the horse's withers. This is very useful for encouraging phlegmatic or reluctant horses to go forward with more energy.

*The body wrap* is an similar idea made of elasticated bandages and, with its reassuring hugging feel, it calms those horses who are highly strung, nervous or who habitually go too fast and/or do not readily work in a good posture.

I have often used both items with success and find that horses seem to respond naturally to them.

# LOOSE SCHOOLING

Most horses love loose schooling and most owners enjoy doing it. Unfortunately, in many cases, it consists of people running, waving their arms and shouting, while their horses career around aimlessly. This is *not* what to do. The idea is to increase communication between horse and owner or trainer and this is where body positioning and voice commands really come into their own.

To begin, first lunge your horse normally, then take off his equipment,

Most horses really enjoy working loose. It can be a game as well as a way of enhancing communication between horse and owner, and using the body beneficially and naturally.

except maybe for a headcollar or his lungeing cavesson, and begin again as though lungeing. Of course, he will soon realize that he is free, but he is already in the habit of watching and listening to you. You can use a lungeing whip, a buggy whip or a schooling whip to help you direct your horse, if you wish, but you will probably find that your body position and voice are enough.

With a little practice, you will find that you are almost dancing with your horse and it is often during loose schooling that people discover how much horses enjoy moving with their owners and even copying their movements. You can try lifting your legs high with each step, doing lateral work, going backwards, pirouetting and anything that takes your fancy, and, in no time at all, you could be surprised to see your horse watching and copying you.

Horses watch our every move and you can set the tone of the session, either a quiet time in close contact or a more exciting, playful one – but do not let things get out of control. If your horse does get too silly, just stand perfectly still with your head and shoulders drooped and use your voice to calm him, and he will soon get your message and probably come to you to see what's happening next.

Incidentally, there seems to be an idea around, stemming from some types of natural horsemanship, that you must never look your horse in the eye as he will regard it as aggressive. He will only do this if your posture and facial expression *are* aggressive. Normal, friendly eye contact is actually a big help and horses, I find, expect and want it. So it is fine to look your horse in the eye as you would a friend, and you can be certain that he will be looking at you in the same way. Horses use eye contact with each other all the time.

*Loose schooling for jumping* is quite common and gives the horse a chance to work in a perfectly natural, balanced and unhindered way over obstacles. You can build a special loose-jumping lane if you have the space, or place simple jumps around the perimeter of your arena. If you cannot create a lane, get some friends to stand *quietly* at strategic points to keep the horse out on the track while you send him round with your body and voice. If you all stay calm, keep it brief and use easy obstacles, these sessions will do nothing but good and most horses really enjoy them.

# CHAPTER 8

# The Forward Ethic

This is a short chapter but its subject is absolutely pivotal to the development of a well-schooled riding horse. In fact, along with standing stock-still when asked and not moving until told (which is essential for safety), it is the most important single quality we need to instil into a horse, and which we need to understand fully as riders. It is the true meaning, in relation to riding, of the word 'forward'.

'Forwardness', 'going forward' or 'free, forward movement' all mean the same thing and it is something we hear a lot of in serious riding circles, yet it is a quality which many horses never fully acquire because they are never properly taught it.

## WHAT DOES 'FORWARD' MEAN?

'Forward' means that a horse instantly, unfailingly, reliably, as a matter of habit, responds accurately and with controlled energy to his rider's aids. He doesn't need telling twice. He is a reactor. He is like a car that starts *every* time, like a light which comes on at the flick of a switch and like the sun rising in the morning. You know it's going to happen – it always does. Is your horse like that?

Until a horse is 'going forward' you will get no further because you do not have co-operation, control or 'life' in your riding. You cannot get impulsion (see Chapter 9) which puts the thrill into a horse's gaits, and your horse will trundle, grind, slug or pussyfoot around for ever, carrying you but never transporting you beyond the mundane.

There is another kind of failing to go forward and that is the horse who cruises along nicely and who has natural gaits that are so energetic and free that he gives his rider the *impression* that he is forward, but he only goes forward when he feels like it, not automatically out of habit.

A final misapprehension is that chasing a horse fast round the manège is making him forward. It is not. It is just making him go fast. As explained above, 'forward' is a state of mind that is *expressed* in free, willing movement – it is not a *product* of movement. Excessive speed for the gait being performed destroys the horse's enjoyment, whatever natural cadence he may have, his balance and therefore his lightness, his confidence in himself and his rider and his progress in schooling. Don't fall for it.

The title of this chapter is The Forward Ethic. Even if horses do not understand ethics, we do. It is we riders who need The Forward Ethic, not our horses, who must simply become confirmed in the habit of forwardness. Forwardness must govern our entire approach to riding, schooling, training and handling our horses.

When I was a child, my first riding master once asked me for a definition of 'forward'. I remember replying, smugly, that it meant a horse who *moves* when you give the leg aid. I was well squashed when my teacher said 'No' and moved on to ask the next pupil in the line-up. I cannot remember what she said, but at the end of the 10-minute verbal lesson which we had in the middle of every class, he gave us his definition which I have never forgotten. He said: 'It describes a horse who is always ready and willing to obey *instantly* whatever aid his rider gives.' He went on to explain that a horse can be 'forward' when standing still, moving laterally or even reining-back because the *mental impetus* is there. And that is what it is all about.

## THE BACKGROUND TO FORWARDNESS

When dealing in any way with your horse, you should, from the very beginning, have *instantly* praised every correct response to an aid from you, whether vocal or physical, and *instantly* ceased the aid completely when he has responded so that he has learnt the association. You should also have corrected *instantly* every misdemeanour or failure to respond when you knew for certain that the horse understood the situation and was capable of doing what you asked, not declining because of uncertainty or distress of some kind.

With this kind of upbringing as his foundation, with his 'Yes' and 'No' boundaries well in place both on the ground and under saddle, forwardness is not difficult to teach. It is true that some horses are phlegmatic or even appear lazy but it is not horse-friendly to keep allowing sluggish responses to aids. If this applies to your horse and you do not correct it, if ever he goes to another owner or is ridden by someone else in your absence, he may suffer much worse treatment at their hands than anything *you* deliver. This is likely to take the form of more and repeated pressure, perhaps severe and often applied randomly (with bad timing), which cannot possibly form an association in the horse's mind and which might amount to abuse.

## INSTILLING FORWARDNESS

So, let's imagine that your horse's responses to your aids (vocal or physical) need crisping up. If you are sure you can discount all genuine reasons for non-compliance, consider trying the following:

- Apply your (correctly applied and timed) aids (voice and body) and, if he does not respond promptly, repeat them a little more strongly until he does – then stop them *absolutely at once* so that the association is formed in his mind – Pressure (aid) → Response → No pressure.

  *If the pressure/aid does not stop the instant he responds, his brain will not learn that reacting to the aid relieves the pressure (because, in his mind, it hasn't) and it will be his sluggish response, if any, which is confirmed rather than forwardness, because nothing you have done has taught him any differently.* He will also probably have become confused and maybe rather disgruntled or worried because he does not understand what is happening to him.

  When you have your desired response, continue riding for some seconds giving no aids but, by all means, praising him with your voice, then walk on a free rein. Then repeat the process, and so on, until the response is confirmed in one session. Be faultless in ceasing the aid when he responds and generous in your praise. You should notice a real difference in only two or three attempts. Next time you ride, he should be sharper but, if not, repeat as above. You will find that, if you are consistent in your technique and timing, he *will* become habitually forward and this will be simple to transfer to whatever you ask him to do. (If whoever else rides him does *not* do this, he will become confused and behave accordingly.)

Here are some other techniques to try.

- Apply your aids and, if he does not respond crisply, apply them again and, with your whip hand off the rein, give him a *light tap* with your schooling whip immediately behind the leg giving the aid (or the inside leg if you are using both legs), to emphasize their action. If you need to repeat the process, as described above, you can slightly strengthen the tap but *never under any circumstances* hurt the horse. Repeat, cease the aid immediately and praise as above.
- Your horse should have learnt on the lunge what the lungeing whip means, so he should be used to responding to its being pointed at his hindquarters, or to the thong being snaked behind him near the ground, by moving forward more energetically. As you ride, have a sensible, knowledgeable assistant nearby with a lungeing whip and, if you need to repeat your aids, ask your assistant to point the whip at his quarters *as you aid the horse* so that he is in no doubt that he must wake up. If he still does not do so, your assistant should snake the thong behind him until he does, without touching him. Again, repeat, cease the aid and praise, as appropriate.
- Many horses respond to a whip just being carried or waved down their sides. Also, try tapping your boot with it, rather than the horse. Clicking with your tongue may be frowned on by some but it does help to have a unique sound to associate with generally 'electrifying' your horse, whether it is clicking, 'Go on' or making a half-whistling or whooshing sound, which I find pretty successful.

Remember – the object is to make forwardness a habit with the horse.

## EXCEPTIONAL CIRCUMSTANCES

The points made in this chapter about instilling forwardness should pertain to all normal circumstances but, as in all matters equestrian, we need to be prepared to acknowledge and deal with abnormal situations, should they arise.

On one extreme, we must always remember that the horse is a prey animal and his survival instinct (even in domesticated horses) is very strong

Reiner Klimke schooling a young horse in medium canter: the horse is happy, balanced and 'forward'.

– and may even be irresistible if a horse is frightened enough. In such circumstances, the scales can tip in favour of terror and panic reactions such as bolting. While this may involve extreme 'going forward' (away from the source of fear), this is patently not the 'forwardness' of a horse 'ready and willing to obey *instantly* whatever aid his rider gives'. Indeed, in a state of overriding panic, the horse may not even register normal aids. Confronted with such circumstances, you can simply do your best to stay on and try to control him with body and voice whilst he is being the horse that nature created. It is my view that, *if the immediate  environs allow for it in relative safety*, a rider confronted with such a situation is better off letting the horse run for a modest distance before making significant efforts to control him. This may allow the initial response to the fright reaction/adrenalin surge to subside. As a reinforcement of what 'forwardness' means, a horse who is usually 'forward' in the desired sense, and who has confidence in his rider, is likely to 'calm down' *more quickly* in the aftermath of such a situation than one who is not.

The converse to the extreme just mentioned is when a horse lacks forwardness for reasons that are initially unclear. There are times in all our lives when we just don't feel very well, when we have a splitting headache, when some part of our body is hurting, when we feel sick or have indigestion, when we have no surplus energy at all – and there are a myriad other reasons for not wanting, or feeling able, to do something. Horses are mammals like us and they function, basically, very like us. Some people say that because horses are not human they cannot have feelings like us. I am not sure whether they really believe this or are using it as an excuse for making a horse work to order.

The fact is that horses most certainly do feel pain, discomfort, distress, fear, illness and lack of well-being, and any of these are excellent reasons for not wanting or being able to go forward. As a caring owner, you will probably develop (or have developed) a reliable 'sixth sense' about how your horse is feeling. Common horse sense is also a major advantage. If you just *know* that something is not right, even though you cannot put your finger on it at the moment, it is wise to accept his reluctance when he declines to go forward and not to ride him at all until you have got to the bottom of his problem. If a normally active, compliant horse is sluggish, it is a certainty that something is wrong. Of course, one of the advantages of having a normally 'forward' horse is that it will be more immediately obvious if he is not so, than would be the case with a habitually sluggish horse.

CHAPTER 9

# Riding From Back to Front

The title of this chapter does not mean that we need to get our principles the wrong way round! It means that we need to become more concerned with what our horse is doing with his hindquarters and legs than with how he looks in front. So very many riders are front-end oriented when actually we all need to be very much back-end oriented.

The reason for this is that the horse's energy and forward impetus are produced in his hindquarters and legs. These are where the powerful pushing muscles are sited, and the way these are developed by the work we give him and the way in which the horse uses them are fundamental to a correct way of going. These muscles push the horse along, or up over fences, and they also perform a broadly similar lifting function in the elevated and weight-bearing steps of collection. In a riding horse of any kind, they need to be strengthened by correct and fair, graduated work to enable the horse to carry not only his own weight but also that of his rider. As with any athlete, physical development takes time but, done correctly and humanely, it gives a horse a much better chance of a long working life with less chance of sustaining injuries. In order to facilitate correct development, it is useful to have a basic understanding of 'how the horse works' (referred to as his biomechanics).

# THE SKELETON AND SPINAL MOVEMENT

The bony framework of the skeleton determines the horse's conformation. Ligaments help to hold the skeleton together. Ligament tissue is strong but more or less inelastic, with very little 'give' in it. It is poorly supplied with blood (so takes a long time to heal) but richly supplied with nerves (so ligament injuries are extremely painful). The development of the skeleton requires proper feeding from foal-hood: indeed, it starts in the womb, so the dam needs correct feeding, too.

Bone is hard but not rigid and is subject to alteration in its size and density according to nutrition and to the stresses it receives. Moderate amounts of stress (movement and pressure) stimulate it to increase in size and strengthen, but too much causes injury to its structure – although diseases, particularly osteoarthritis, can also do this. The ends of bones are protected from friction and pressure to some extent by gristly cartilage, which is subject to the same stresses from work and disease as the bone itself.

The horse's brain is his main 'control centre' and its continuation, the spinal cord, runs along inside the spinal column. This column is made up of variously shaped individual bones called vertebrae, each with a hole in its centre, so the whole line of vertebrae forms a tube or tunnel which carries the spinal cord. The vertebrae have protective pads or discs of cartilage between them, and nerves branch out from the spinal cord between the vertebrae to nearly all parts of the body.

The shape of the spine forms a very slight upward (convex) arch when seen from the side. This is a stronger structure from the viewpoint of carrying weight than a straight-line formation and certainly much stronger than a slightly dipped (concave) one. The horse's heavy abdominal contents are supported by soft tissue from the underside of the spine and the upper parts of the ribs, so there is already a downward pull on the spine. The addition of a saddle and rider, and a moving rider at that (movement always intensifies the effect of weight), creates a further downward influence on the spine.

The horse's spine is not nearly so flexible as people in the horse world used to think. The most flexible parts are the neck and tail: there is very little flexibility in the rest of the spine, just a little upward/downward and sideways flexion. This, also, varies somewhat from section to section. For example, the five vertebrae of the quarters behind the croup are fused together, forming the sacrum, and are incapable of any flexion at all. The sacrum forms very tight joints with the underneath of the two ilia ('wing bones') of the pelvis, those joints being called the sacro-iliac joints which, again, permit a very tiny amount of movement.

When the horse moves, his spine (taken as a whole) arches and dips a little, this being most noticeable in moments of suspension and when the horse lands from them, when it arches and dips respectively. It is easy to imagine the significant effect a poor rider banging about on the horse's back, or riding out of balance, can have on his comfort and soundness.

## MUSCLES AND TENDONS

While the skeleton represents the basic structure of the horse, the powerhouses behind it, which move the bones and thus the horse himself, are the muscles and their attached tendons.

Muscle is very sensitive 'meat' tissue with excellent supplies of blood and nerves; therefore, muscle injuries can be extremely painful but heal well with correct treatment. The tendons which attach muscles mainly to bones are extensions of the muscle tissue but, although tendon tissue has a good nerve supply it has a very poor blood supply, so again, like ligament tissue, injuries are painful and take a long time to heal.

It is the nerves spreading out from the spinal cord all around the body which control the action of muscles. Messages pass back and forth along the nerves by means of electrical impulses and chemical transmitters, informing the spinal cord and brain of conditions affecting the muscles such as pain from cramp or injury, sensations of heat or cold, and of their biochemical condition as regards the presence or absence of nutrients and fuel, and waste products produced during work. Muscles also receive messages via the nerves about when and how to move for the purposes of work (and all muscle movement is work), and for relief when they are tired or have been in one position too long.

A simple description of how muscles work is to think of a muscle as being attached to a stable bone at one end by means of short tendon tissue and to a different bone at the other by means of a longer tendon, the two bones being linked by a joint between them. The muscle, in response to a nervous message, will shorten and fatten (contract), pulling on the second bone which is moved as a result, while the joint in between them flexes.

Muscles work in opposing pairs (or groups). When a muscle contracts, its opposing partner is stretched and lengthened but it always stays in slight opposing tension (contraction) to control its partner's action, which is still active work. This normally prevents injury to tissues, which might otherwise be caused by overstretching them, and prevents joints being over-flexed. Whether they are contracting directly or maintaining tension in opposition, muscles develop in size and become stronger by working like this. A knowledgeable horseman/woman can tell just by looking at a horse's muscular development whether or not he has been worked correctly.

The body responds to work or stress by building up tissue (including bone, which is also sensitive to stresses); correct work, gradually increased, produces a horse with a developed, balanced musculature who is in good control of his own body and able to use it to best advantage.

Muscle is a protein tissue which also contains sugar in the form of glycogen for energy production and work. Oxygen, delivered to the muscles via the respiratory system and bloodstream (which also delivers nutrients), is stored there in the muscle protein pigment, myoglobin. In the process known as aerobic respiration, glycogen and oxygen react to produce energy, and the major waste product, carbon dioxide, is removed in the bloodstream and expelled via the lungs. During hard, sustained work or fast, power work, the muscles can use up oxygen faster than the heart and lungs can supply it in the bloodstream. In these circumstances, there is greater reliance on a different type of muscle fibres and energy is produced by a process known as anaerobic respiration. When this occurs, a waste product called lactic acid is produced. This is usually removed via the bloodstream but, in demanding circumstances, production can occur faster than it can be removed, and the lactic acid can build up in the muscles, creating acidosis, a condition that impairs muscle function and causes fatigue and pain.

Thus we can see that horses' muscles can do prolonged work at slow to moderate speeds for much longer periods without getting tired than they can do fast or power work such as galloping, jumping or hard gymnastic work such as schooling. Muscles which are not allowed to rest adequately become tired, weak and painful – in extreme cases, to the extent that they, and the body of which they are constituents, simply cannot continue to work.

It may be hard to imagine this end result occurring during a schooling session in a manège but horses can go a long way down this road if they are worked for too long, too hard, too fast, are performing physically taxing movements or are working in ways that require them to maintain a particular outline (which is significant muscular work) without giving the muscles (not to mention the heart and lungs) frequent enough and long enough breaks. Such work does not develop muscles beneficially; it injures them and is inhumane. It is not clever or correct, good practice to bring a horse out of a manège soaked in sweat and heaving for breath, yet some people feel that a horse has not worked 'adequately' if this does not happen.

A knock-on effect of such work is that horses in physical discomfort will try to use other muscles, as well as various physical contortions if they possibly can, to try to escape it. This can result in incorrect development of the 'wrong' muscles and also injury to them and perhaps to other tissues, too. (The example given later this chapter – see Engagement – shows that long-term nerve damage is also likely to be caused by enforced, unnatural postures.)

## Rest and Relaxation

Muscles can be rested during a work session by allowing the horse a few minutes to either walk around on a completely loose rein or just stand still, also on a free rein (provided he is not too warm and it is not a chilly day). Even the gentle contact of a long (as opposed to loose) rein is sufficiently inhibiting to prevent the horse from stretching his head and neck down freely to relieve his body, taking long, loose strides and really relaxing. So really let your reins go: they should be long enough to let your horse's muzzle reach the ground whilst you are sitting up straight holding them by the buckle.

When muscles are relaxing correctly, the blood can pass easily through their loose tissues, bringing nutrients and oxygen and clearing away waste. This process is essential for muscle health and optimal function. There is also the big advantage to the horse – and maybe the rider! – of a few minutes mental R&R, just chilling out and not having to think about much.

## The 'Ring of Muscles'

Since muscles are needed to move bones, it is obvious that they are involved in the process of engagement, which we will consider in the next section. The muscles, tendons and ligaments around the horse's body which produce the beneficial outline we want (according to the different stages of the horse's schooling), are together known as the Ring of Muscles. This ring comprises structures along the top-line, beginning at the poll and running along the neck, withers, back, loins and hindquarters, then those around the pelvis and thigh bones, the abdominal or belly muscles, the breastbone, the underside of the neck and then back to the poll. This combination of muscles, tendons and ligaments is attached to the related skeletal bones, forming a continuous connection of tissues and structures all around the horse.

When the horse is worked appropriately, gradually learning to tuck the bottom of his pelvis forward and under, lifting his belly by contracting his abdominal muscles and stretching his neck forward and down (or up, if he is more advanced), the ring results in the horse appearing shortened along his underside and lengthened and rounded along his top-line. As you can imagine from the foregoing explanation, this is hard work for an unfit horse of any age, but particularly for a young one. Even athletically fit horses not used to adopting this posture – racehorses, for instance – find it hard, but it must be done in short spells to get them used to it, gradually increasing to a very few minutes. As your guide, just think of how few minutes a Preliminary (or Training level) dressage test lasts (between 4 and 5 minutes approximately, including a 'rest' period of walk on a free rein) and this should confirm to you that drilling horses round for an over-long schooling session of 30 to 60 minutes, whether ridden or from the ground, and without plenty of rests, is grossly overdoing things and can cause both physical and psychological harm.

Initially, the horse will only be able to hold the posture for a very few *seconds* and you must use sensitivity and judgement when asking him to spend longer in it. He hardly uses it at all in nature so the muscles involved will be weak, but since he does need to develop them for safe weight-carrying, you need to work them for carefully increased lengths of time.

# ENGAGEMENT

In skeletal terms, it is the lumbo-sacral joint (the crucial joint between the front of the sacrum and the last lumbar vertebra) which allows the horse to 'tuck his bottom under', perform a 'pelvic tuck' or 'engage his hindquarters'. Thus the flexion of this joint is what we need for the engagement of the hindquarters. Because the hind legs are joined to the pelvis at the hip joints, when the pelvis tucks under, the huge thigh bones and the rest of the hind legs are brought more under the horse, enabling him to push effectively, and the hindquarters are said to be 'engaged'. This skeletal movement is facilitated by the correct action of the 'ring of muscles', described earlier.

All good riders and trainers allow their horses the time to develop, and take the time to school and strengthen them both on the ground and under saddle, so that they can learn to engage effectively and incrementally, starting with the posture known as 'long-and-low' (see next section).

If the trouble is not taken and the time not allowed to enable this correct process of development, the horse is put in real danger of sustaining injury to the soft tissues (muscles and other tissues) of his back and to the bones and cartilage of his spine because his back *will* sag under the weight of a rider, destroying its natural arch shape. The hind legs and quarters also suffer stress, strain and injuries because they are working in an unnatural angulation and posture, and  they are also disengaged and trailing out behind the horse, where their pushing power is greatly reduced.

However, in an attempt to speed up this process, many people adopt the practice of enforcing a head-carriage on the horse (riding him the wrong way, from front to back), as if this will automatically bring with it all the other physical requirements of a schooled horse. It has to be said that many of these riders do not understand the back-to-front principle or the importance of hind-end thrust or, indeed, the inescapable fact that rushing the schooling and production process does not produce a physically correct, mentally willing and educated horse. It is really bad practice for a horse to be held 'up and in' in a pseudo-advanced outline at any age, whether on the ground or under saddle, and it invites physical injury to the neck and shoulder tissues. Since this damaging practice is very common at the time of writing and publication of this book, I would like to give just one, real-life example of its effects.

I was recently talking to the owner of a young, potential competition horse who engaged a professional trainer to visit and school him a few days a week, hacking him out herself in between times. On arrival at the owner's yard, the youngster was beautifully mannered, his basic work in place, he was trusting of people and easy to handle. The trainer announced that the horse was ready to go on to more advanced work and needed to start developing his outline. On every visit, he was ridden on a very firm contact with his head and neck fixed up and in and taken round the school in a strong trot for almost an hour, with no significant break. The owner did query this but the trainer, who was well-known and highly recommended, told her that it was what the horse needed.

The horse soon started showing behavioural problems under saddle and on the ground. He became distrustful of people (not only the trainer), bargy, very head-shy, hard-mouthed and spooky out hacking, to the point at which the owner was afraid to ride and even to handle him. She could not get a headcollar on him without trouble, and could not bridle him at all. As the trainer was away, she took the opportunity to call in the vet. After a preliminary examination, the vet gave the opinion that the horse had been worked in draw-reins. The owner described what the trainer had been doing and the vet explained to the owner the problems which this type of abuse causes. Further investigations revealed damage to the nerves in the neck all the way down from the poll owing to compression where they left the spinal cord between the vertebrae. He advised a year's complete break from work, with a reassessment at the end of that time, but the outlook is not promising.

The correct and humane way to school any horse is to allow him the time, years, in fact, to build up gradually and, if young, to do his natural growing, developing and maturing as well. Making gradually increasing, gentle demands on him *as he masters each stage and shows by his performance, physique and attitude that he is comfortable and ready to move on* will result in the contented, confident, well-schooled and developed horse described earlier in this chapter.

## Working Long-and-low

The act of going long-and-low, with the horse's head and neck stretched out and down, enables the horse to move as we want at an early stage, with the back/spine encouraged to lift, the abdominal muscles to contract and strengthen and the quarters and hind legs to come under a little. The position of the head and neck also enables him to use these parts freely to balance himself as he learns and gets used to this gymnastic work. You can see this when horses trot this way in the field for a few seconds, tracking up more and swinging along naturally.

This posture also intensifies the natural, slight, upward arch of the spine into what is known as the *'vertebral bow'* because the spine can be likened to a bow shape (as in archery). Because an upward arch, as used in a bridge-building, is a strong structure from a weight-carrying point of view, we seek to develop this way of going in a riding horse, strengthening his muscles and other tissues in response to careful, correct work, because it makes it easier for him to carry not only his own heavy abdominal contents but the weight of a rider and saddle as well, all of which are exerting a downward force on the spine.

As horses strengthen up and experience the feeling of their bodies in this posture, they clearly enjoy springing and swinging along and adopt it willingly and easily. With time and tactful schooling, almost any horse, conformation permitting, can move on towards the stage at which his neck stretches forward and *up* and he works easily and comfortably with his poll the highest point of his outline (except for his ears) and the front of his face just in front of the vertical, as set out in all the classical and most respected books on correct schooling and equitation. However, as mentioned this *must* be a gradual process.

With a young, unfit or badly schooled horse, or one returning from injury, you need to start work in the long-and-low posture for 10 to 20 minutes maximum (including frequent rests on a free rein) initially on alternate days and later on most days, like a fitness programme. The horse can start learning about this kind of work dismounted, as detailed in Chapter 7, so he will understand the posture when you begin ridden work. Of course, the unaccustomed weight on his back will initially cause it to sag a little; at the same time and as part of the same effect, the head and neck will tend to come up and out and the hind legs to trail or be disengaged. This concave posture makes it more difficult for the horse to raise his back and belly but correct work, in itself, strengthens him if done sensibly. It is always a good idea to start with the lightest, most competent rider you can find.

To ask the horse to go with 'both ends down and the middle up' in the long-and-low posture, first lunge or long-rein him as usual in this posture for just a few minutes before mounting. Check that he responds to the 'head down' verbal command in case you need it. Check also that his noseband is loose enough to enable him to flex the joint of his jaw to the bit, rather than just flexing at the poll, and that his bit is fitted comfortably, as described earlier.

It also helps if he already understands the rein aid for flexing at the jaw and poll, and you can teach him this from the ground. In the stable, stand by his head and hold the reins under his throat in a riding position. Choose one to be your outside and one to be your inside rein. Take a firm but gentle contact (see Chapter 5) on the outside rein and, with the inside one, give on–off squeezes on the rein to create intermittent gentle but present pressure on the inside of his lower jaw. (Some horses respond better to an intermittent vibration of the inside rein rather than a squeeze.)

It will not take the horse long to give to the bit by slightly opening his mouth, flexing at the joint of his jaw and flexing at the poll, to avoid the pressure. The very instant he does this, stop the aid (because he has given you what you asked for), praise him but *do not* draw your hands back with his mouth. He has responded to your aid and has lightened the contact through flexion at poll and jaw, which is absolutely correct, so if you then maintain the contact at the same pressure by drawing back your hands, he has learnt nothing. Repeat this then do it from the other side.

An additional aid you can use to help is to get him used to a vocal command for flexion which does not sound like any other you use, possibly 'Give' or 'Flex'. Of course, he will not understand it yet, but say it at the very instant he flexes – and every time – so that he associates the sound with the action and soon, as with any other vocal aid, you will be able to say it during work and he will give to the bit unless he is uncomfortable or having problems.

Once he begins to comply, take him to a couple of different places on the yard and repeat the whole procedure so that he does not associate it with only one place. Then take him into the manège and do the same. Then do it in walk from both sides, maybe with the assistance of a friend on the ground to help keep him walking.

I should emphasize that this apparent concentration on the front end is in no way a version of riding from front to back. Once mounted, you are going to use your leg aids to send him forward into a reasonable walk (we are talking about an unfit, green or badly schooled horse here) and many horses, left to their own devices, will then raise their heads to some extent, dropping their backs, allowing their hind legs to trail, yet taking up more bit contact in response to the increased forward activity. *This tense, defensive posture is uncomfortable for them.* I have always found that this simple lesson helps the horse to understand how to go, to flex at poll and jaw and free himself from this concave posture because when the horse loosens up in this way and drops his head, his back is inclined to lift naturally and his hindquarters and legs to come more under. *Then* he will gradually learn, and be able, to round and lighten as a habitual response to his rider's aids. It is rather like turning the key in the lock: it enables him to open the door rather than stay blocked.

Once you are getting the required response consistently from the ground, mount (from a mounting block to save both his back and your saddle) and walk around on a loose rein to start warming him up. Staying in walk, ride straight lines and large circles on both reins, changing direction mainly with your seat and a touch on the outside of his withers as described in Chapter 5, and stay in walk. After a few minutes, take up the reins until you have a feel of his mouth on the bit. Apply the same steady, gentle contact on the outside rein, the same squeezes on the inside rein that you have just used from the ground and the new vocal aid he has just learnt. It is very unlikely that he will not respond as you wish. At first, he may simply give, nod his head down and raise it straightaway. Still praise him and try again several seconds later. Gradually, in this session, ask him to maintain it for a few strides, then give him his head on a loose rein.

Next, send him forward a little more actively into your hands, asking for more hind leg activity and reach, then ask him to give again. Don't use your legs and hands at the same moment. He will be getting the idea by now. Remember to keep your hands and legs still and quiet when he responds, and to praise him. He should maintain a gentle but present contact on the bit, so make sure that it is there for him. Try a few strides in rising trot in the same way. As this is enough for one day, stop there and try again another day. He will fairly soon understand that this is his working posture and be happy to adopt it if you also give him lots of rest breaks.

Some trainers advise that the contact be kept stable and that the horse will flex and lighten up of his own accord, in time, in response to the increased activity of the hind legs and becoming stronger. Some horses *will* do that but some *will not*, even though they may have worked in good posture on the lunge. The latter can learn to lean on or push against the bit, go on the forehand and never develop an educated mouth unless the rider teaches them otherwise. Often, this is because they cannot seem to think of what else to do in response to the rider's forward-driving aids combined with a stable bit contact. If the horse understands being asked to flex to the bit and at the poll before you mount, it is much easier to get this response from the saddle. This approach helps you to avoid letting the horse work in a poor posture, so developing the wrong muscles as you wait for the penny to drop. His time under saddle should be spent in a good posture or resting and relaxing on a loose rein, not resisting your aids and developing all the wrong muscles by going badly.

Working long-and-low can be done over poles, both on the ground and raised a little, and also on slightly sloping ground – both up and down the slope. This really encourages hind leg activity, engagement and a beneficial working posture. In time, as the horse strengthens, you will feel him maintaining the posture but volunteering to use his hindquarters and legs more, bring his neck more up and arched forward whilst still being happy to accept your gentle, reliable contact, also responding to your inside rein requests, as appropriate. Your horse is then learning, from an early stage in his schooling, to develop self-balance and a safe, independent but co-operative way of going.

You want to produce a horse who will voluntarily hold this posture on a light bit contact without being constantly asked for it or driven into it. He will only learn this if you teach him correctly. This produces a horse with a lovely mouth and a rare freedom in his action and comfort in his body. His gaits are naturally enhanced, not exaggeratedly forced; he can look after his rider and himself because he can use his natural balance rather than have it destroyed (along with his spirit and agility) by having the balancing pole of his head and neck clamped in a vice-like grip.

## INCORRECT PRACTICE

What you do *not* want to produce (I hope) is a horse who is held up and in by means of a hard, rigid bit contact (in the guise of 'support'), made worse by a tight noseband and too tight and high a bit ('to teach him to accept the bit'), causing untold injury, pain and distress. Of course, this is cruel – even though some people do not accept that.

At no time should a horse be allowed, *and certainly not asked or made*, to duck his head right down and/or bring his nose behind that critical straight, vertical line from forehead to ground, commonly known as going 'behind the vertical'. Dropping 'behind' the bit or being overbent have long been regarded as serious faults in riding of any kind and they can be difficult to correct, yet in recent years many trainers and riders have actually encouraged – or even forced – these extreme postures. Horses working in this way are said to be in 'hyperflexion', a posture which the International Equestrian Federation (FEI), the controlling body for international equestrian sport, condemned in April 2008 as being 'mental abuse', confirming that it 'does not support the practice'. As an equine shiatsu therapist, I find it telling that horses I have treated for head, neck, forehand and back pain have almost all been made to go in this way. There is also other evidence that this type of work is harmful and should, therefore, be avoided.

Depending on the horse's head and neck conformation, some find it easy to go in a behind-the-vertical posture and others do not. Those with a natural 'nose-out' conformation (most Thoroughbreds, Arabs and similar types) can be encouraged to carry their noses a *little* more in than natural, in *correct* long-and-low work, and those with a natural head-carriage that is closer to the vertical may be asked to come *just* on to it at most. The slight effort of this exercise enhances the functioning of the ring of muscles. The important points for the trainer to look for and for the rider to feel are the lifting of the back and belly and the lowering of the hindquarters, with the hind legs being used actively from the hips and being brought well under the belly.

You may hear some trainers and riders say of a horse that they do not mind if he is ridden on or behind the vertical all or most of the time because 'he is that kind of horse and he goes that way naturally'. 'Naturally' can only mean at complete liberty in the field. Do they mean that their horse carries himself on and behind the vertical in the field as his normal posture other than when grazing? I have spent all my life around horses and have never seen one go that way usually and *naturally* other than when giving a momentary toss and twirl of the head when playing or focusing to look at something close up, and this includes Iberians and those modern competition Warmbloods specifically bred to be more 'up and in'. (In the unlikely event that I came across a horse who had the kind of conformation which meant that it was normal for him to stand, walk, trot and canter with his head behind the vertical when free in the field, I would say he was a freak and did not have suitable conformation for a riding horse.) If a horse does *not* do it as his normal posture in the field but does it when ridden, it is obviously an aspect of how he is ridden that makes him do it, and that can only be the rider.

## *Working the More Advanced Horse*

When a correctly worked horse's muscles are building up, he feels stronger, better balanced and more confident. His outline will be changing a little, his forehand coming up a bit, his head and neck are still stretching forward but coming up a little in response to his change in balance, his hindquarters will be engaging readily and his weight be taken back a little more on to them. He is, of course, calm in his work – and 'forward'!

### PRAPARING FOR IMPULSION

This is the time to *gradually* start asking for impulsion, that exhilarating surge of power from the hindquarters and hind legs which gives the rider the sensation of being pushed forward and lifted up from behind by an irresistible power source (the power source being the horse's 'engine' – his engaged hindquarters and legs with their powerful muscles).

Producing impulsion is hard work for your horse and he needs to have his strength increased by various means. Hill work is wonderful if it is available in your locality. Working uphill develops pushing power and work downhill enhances engagement. Go up and down initially gentle slopes with sound footing, in a straight line. Working in water just below knee level also makes the legs and joints more active. Lengthening and shortening of stride and transitions from gait to gait, properly done, bring the horse 'into hand', causing him to use himself rather than just cruise along. Shoulder-fore and shoulder-in also strengthen and supple the horse, and teach him to push forward from engaged hindquarters and hind legs. Finally, work over poles both on the ground and slightly raised in all three gaits works his muscles harder and makes him watch where he is putting his feet, thereby strengthening him and improving his agility and his thinking ability. Poles can also be used, carefully, in shortening and lengthening the stride.

## IMPULSION

As mentioned earlier, many people mistake speed for impulsion. The difference between speed and impulsion as far as the feeling you get is concerned is that there is no *upward* thrust in mere speed. You simply feel that you are being carried forward with energy but you may have a niggling feeling that all is not

This horse is well balanced but in a nondescript posture and not 'going anywhere' or working his body particularly beneficially.

The same horse swinging along in a positive and focused way, in good balance and posture, active and doing himself no end of good.

as it should be – and you will be right. Too fast a speed for the gait ('running') can be used by a horse as a means of avoiding the hard, muscular work of producing engagement and impulsion. On the other hand, if he does not entirely understand your aids (always rider error) he will produce speed because he thinks that is what to do. Speed also can be demanded by a trainer or rider who does not understand the meaning and purpose of impulsion or how to get it. The end result is the same. (Of course, an able, well-developed and well-trained horse can travel fast *with* genuine impulsion – that is to say the two qualities are not mutually exclusive – but if such a horse is driven 'off his feet' he, too, will lose the impulsive quality of his movement.)

The horse going too fast is usually too much on the forehand, which overburdens his forelegs; also, instead of arching and reaching his forelegs forward from the shoulders, he will probably go with a straight-legged, hoof-flicking action which stresses the tendons, ligaments and joints. Excessive speed puts a horse out of balance so he may well take too strong a contact on the bit and go with his back and belly down and hind legs trailing. He stiffens up, is anxious or actually frightened. This is all completely counter-productive to the calm, strong and confident horse we are aiming for.

## How to Ask for Impulsion

Straight lines being easier than circles, start on a long side of your school so that your horse has plenty of room in front of him and is not inhibited by soon coming to a corner. (Of course, you can ask for impulsion out in the open but be careful that it does not degenerate into mere speed.) Establish a rhythmic, working trot (rising) for his early attempts, on his preferred diagonal, with engagement, and *relax* in your mind and body. All you are going to do now is ask your horse to go forward a little more purposefully and energetically into your normal light contact with a gentle, passive resistance on your outside rein.

With soft seat and legs, have a *slightly* forward angle to your upper body *from the hip joints*, not the waist (as the latter would make you crouch). This takes your weight a little off his hindquarters and encourages him to lift his back. You want to activate his hind legs, so bring your legs back a little from the hips (not just the knees) and squeeze with them in time with his rhythm. Squeeze with the calf on the side on which a hind leg is lifting – as the right hind comes forward, squeeze with your right calf, and vice versa. If necessary, check by looking down at his shoulders to start you off: as his right hind comes forward, his right shoulder will come back, and vice versa. In rising trot, this means that you should squeeze with one calf on the rise and with the other on the sit. This gives a very clear aid to your horse to activate the relevant hind leg. If you perform the minimalist rising trot described earlier (Chapter 5) with a forward-sit movement rather than an up-down one, you will not find this too difficult. As he strengthens up – and provided you can do a really soft, absorbing sitting trot, you will find it easier to use the same aiding technique in that gait.

*DO NOT:*

- Keep your legs on in a constant contact. The squeezes need to give your horse an on-off feel in time with his rhythm and on the same side as the hind leg moving forward. (If alternate legs make him 'rock', use both legs.)
- Let your legs flap in and out as you give your aids as this disconcerts many horses and puts them off balance.
- Allow the tempo (speed) to increase. Keep the rhythm determinedly regular with your rise, being prepared to slow it down fractionally if the horse speeds it up.

If your horse's preceding work has been correct and he is ready for impulsion, he will almost certainly respond by stepping more actively with his hind legs as he emphasizes the engagement of his hindquarters. You will feel his back lift and the energy surge through his body into your hands where you hold and direct it gently like the precious gift it is.

You may not get the whole effect the first few times you try, but at this stage the horse is trying to work out how to respond, so be delighted with about three or four strides, then relax your aids and let him cruise for a few steps before trying again. Praise him generously the instant you feel the upward thrust being generated in his quarters. Once he understands impulsion, you will be able to ask for it and leave him to it, not having to constantly aid him with your legs.

Impulsion will, in itself, strengthen and balance the horse further, taking you gradually towards …

## COLLECTION

True collection with the horse in correct self-carriage on the weight of the rein is the aim of every discerning horseman/woman.

It is a state in which the horse takes more weight on to his hindquarters, with lowered and flexed croup (lumbo-sacral joint) and hind legs, raised back, belly and forehand and with his neck arched and stretched forwards and up, flexing at the jaw to a suggestion from the bit and at the poll, which must be the highest point of his outline. The front of his face should be just in front of or, at most, *on* the vertical, depending on how his head is set naturally on to his neck. Those horses who do not have a loose, open and arched throat conformation should not be asked to flex too much at the poll as it will cause them discomfort, or even pain.

In collection, the horse is more 'gathered together' and *appears* shorter in his body from front to back, NOT because he is being held in to simulate the mere appearance of collection, but because he is assuming it after a few years of being carefully strengthened, developed and mentally habituated to moving with self-control, and the *freedom* to see ahead comfortably and to express his gaits to the best of his ability.

The feeling for the rider is one of absolute ecstasy and there is every reason to believe that the horse feels great as well. Your hands feel almost redundant as you maintain and guide your horse mainly with your seat and legs. He is maintaining the collected posture voluntarily on the weight of an extremely light or hanging, silken rein, so all you have to do is sit there and ask for whatever movements you want – provided he has been trained to do them, of course.

Collection is the ultimate in riding from back to front. You feel as though you are balanced on the horse's hind end, growing up out of your horse, and he will move at the merest aid or nuance of a change of weight or position – little more than a thought from you. Forwardness, engagement and impulsion are all combined synergistically to produce something wonderful, something that Nuno Oliveira, surely the greatest classical rider and trainer of the twentieth century, described as 'the heaven of horsemen'. What a terrific expression!

The more you experience true collection the more you realize that it cannot possibly come from any kind of coercion whatsoever. Bad riders can pull a horse in, strap him up and down, drive him forward, drill him until he's in a muck sweat and grind their aids into him until both individuals – for this is never a partnership – are exhausted, but they will never attain collection.

Collection results from the systematic, correct development of the horse's body and the way he uses it. It is not only a priceless prize for the rider but also a gift to the horse – a gift of a strong, capable body, a calm, free and individual mind and a promise of a long, sound life. Properly schooled horses are, in my experience, much less likely to be injured by their normal work and so do not suffer the pain and malcontentment of horses worked less considerately and who are regularly injured and off work. Correct schooling and the development of a horse's natural physique to enhance his normal action is the only horse-friendly way to go, if we are going to ride horses.

Not every horse, pony or rider will have the potential to attain full collection but many more than we may imagine could reach the early levels of it. This does demand from the rider a level of commitment and dedication plus the realization that only humane, correct, proven schooling methods will do the job. Enjoyment and fulfilment come with this attitude and it does all seem to rub off on to the horse. Horses definitely know when they have a place in life, a job, a human partner, trainer and carer, even if they do not think of their situation in those human terms, and I am certain that they are reassured by it.

CHAPTER 10

# Calm, Forward and Straight

The title of this chapter is a very famous saying in the horse world, forever linked to General Alexis-Francois L'Hotte (1825–1904) (see Further Reading). General L'Hotte was a consummate French cavalry officer, *écuyer* and writer, his book *Questions Équestres* (Equestrian Questions), published posthumously in 1906, still being a classic bible for riders of any discipline, on any type of horse. 'Calm, forward and straight' has long been a basic principle of French equitation and is still a reliable watch-phrase for all riders today. The elements it contains are the foundation stones on which everything else is built and without which you cannot achieve lightness – the proof of the pudding.

The order in which these three key conditions are set out is invariable and totally reliable. You will start off on the right foot if you ensure that each is mastered before you move on, and return to them when problems arise.

## CALMNESS

Calmness and relaxation can only come about when the horse feels he has nothing to worry about. This is a basic tenet of his life. Thus calmness and relaxation are absolute requisites for any horse before any other work or schooling can be absorbed. The horse must pay full attention to his rider and be confident in doing so in order for him to assess the aids and respond appropriately, or for him to be able to absorb new lessons. Therefore, in addition

to having confidence in his rider/trainer, he must be completely comfortable in his body with nothing causing discomfort or irritating him in any way.

Because of his prey-animal mentality, he is easily distracted by anything which might possibly represent danger and is easily upset by anxiety, distress, discomfort and pain. When in the presence of his trusted trainer he should be willing to relax, knowing that nothing frightening or painful ever happens when he is in their company. This places responsibility on his rider/trainer to ensure the horse's physical comfort and mental peace of mind, as far as is humanly possible. In addition, he must not be taken into any situation in which there is a good chance that he will be hurt, stressed or frightened – as far as can possibly be arranged.

## How to Achieve Calmness

Horses relax in the broader sense, in relation to their life in general, when they feel safe in their normal environment, either at home or in familiar places away. Many horses, other than the most seasoned, become uncertain (or worse) when in new places, and few owners nowadays have their horses for all of their lives, so they cannot know what associations their horse is making if he becomes apparently unaccountably frightened, wary, tense or, as General L'Hotte put it so charmingly, 'energetically resistant' in the face of what he sees as a challenging situation.

Ultimately, you want your horse to see you as his trusted companion so that you can work at home or go out and about together, with him looking to you for direction and protection. (In time, the situation may be reversed if he ever becomes a traditional 'schoolmaster' and equine teacher and protector, to use human terms.) This state of affairs normally takes some time to achieve, although it can happen quite quickly. Until then, there are several things you can try to 'keep your horse's head on his shoulders' and minimize the chances of an upset.

At new venues, possibly a competition or when hacking in a new area, try to keep your horse for a while in the company of another he knows well and trusts – or at least gets on with. (Some combinations are like a red rag to a bull and will make a situation even more fraught, but a change of companion can work wonders.) However, when it comes to the working-in phase of a competition, some horses, once initially settled into the venue, will exhibit greater concentration on the rider if they are kept some distance away from other entrants. With many horses, calmness can be promoted by keeping up a steady, soft, undemanding rhythmic trot. Others, however, respond to having their minds kept busy, so with one such as this ask him frequently for movements he does well, change direction, perform transitions from trot to walk and back, and so on. As with people, individual horses in potentially exciting or stressful situations can react in different ways, so the key here is 'get to know your horse'; what works for one may not work so well for another.

If an exciting or worrying situation occurs, try your best to keep your seat and legs quietly adhesive around him, 'hugging' him with your legs but not pressing firmly unless giving a definite aid. Hold them closer together than normal and, again, 'hug' his neck with your hands and reins, keeping a gentle but reassuring level of contact, which you will learn by experience. If he feels you have control of yourself and are not clinging to or grabbing at him, he is more likely to stay calm himself and start to trust you.

When passing frightening objects, 'bend' him around your leg further away from them and, with firm but not harsh aids, do a 'head away' or shoulder-in type of movement, flexed away from the object. This often works very well to keep the horse under reasonable to good control and moving on. It also tells him that (a) you are in control and (b) he needs to pay attention to you which, again, takes his mind off the object somewhat.

In some situations discretion is the better part of valour and it is often the best way forward – literally – to get a lead from a companion instead of sticking to your guns and insisting that your horse learns to go on his own. He will, eventually, but this is a training situation and you need to succeed, so use his herd instincts to your advantage until he 'transfers his loyalties' to you. If things get really bad, you may have no choice, from a safety viewpoint, but to turn back or 'think laterally' and go another route, returning another day when the situation may have changed.

The way in which horses are managed plays a great part in their state of mind. Many these days are fed diets far too high in energy for the work, or merely exercise, they are doing. This makes them prime candidates for seeing 'monsters' behind every bush. Lack of turnout is another reason for this sort of behaviour and general distrust can easily exist between a horse and an owner who never finds time to be with him, to take time over grooming and tacking him up, and who has an air of rushing all the time. How can a horse grow to enjoy or trust someone like this? Horses so often take their cues from us and are excellent 'people readers'. Make sure yours is receiving the right story!

## FORWARDNESS

The quality of forwardness has been discussed in Chapter 8, so you may feel that you want to read it again. Once you have the foundation of Calm, Forward really is the most important aspect of schooling you can work on if you eventually want a reliable, controllable and, therefore, safe mount. All problems of forward movement, from running backwards to bucking, occur because the horse is simply not 'forward' in the schooled sense as a matter of ingrained habit. L'Hotte said: 'The rider must always feel the forward flow of the horse.'

If your horse hesitates *at all* when you give him a familiar aid, he is not forward. Even if he receives an unfamiliar aid, he should immediately do what he *thinks* it means, whether this is move forward, move to the side, slow down, speed up or go backwards.

Forwardness is also necessary for a safely manoeuvrable horse. A horse who does not do what you ask when you ask, is not under safe control and is potentially dangerous. Of course, as with all schooling, it takes time to instil infallible co-operation (obedience or submission, if you prefer those words) but, if you school consistently and correctly, it takes less time than you may think.

As pointed out at the end of Chapter 8, there are times when fear and panic take over and the horse can think of nothing but self-preservation. This is all the more reason to concentrate on achieving habitual forwardness in your schooling so that even if your horse is green in other respects you do, at least, have a reasonably safe ride. The more your horse is confirmed in the forward habit (and, of course, the habit of trusting his rider), the more the prospect of fear triggering his primitive instincts diminishes. It can be a life-saver.

## Balance

Two elements of equitation which go with forwardness are balance and rhythm. Once the horse is going forward more regularly (even if not perfectly habitually), it is easier for him to find balance under the weight of a rider. Of course, he can balance his own body perfectly over any going. You rarely see a free horse fall. It is when a rider gets on that the horse's balance problems start.

A rider's weight is experienced by the horse as being top-heavy and unstable. The horse does not know what the rider might do. If you can imagine how this must feel it will bring home to you the necessity of acquiring a seat which disturbs the horse as little as possible. This is all you can do. You cannot improve the horse's natural, dismounted balance. All you can do is limit the disturbance your weight and actions create until you are, first, moving as one with your horse and, second, able to use your aids to influence your horse whilst maintaining that ability.

L'Hotte emphasized that we should do less to enable our horses to do more, and better. Most riders are too active and some teachers actually tell their students that they should be doing something at every stride. A principal classical tenet is to ask your horse to do something, then let him do it by being passive, and then ask him to do something different. By maintaining your position for whatever movement you have asked for, the schooled horse knows to keep doing it and you only need to intervene if the quality of the movement deteriorates. So give your horse a chance – which is the title of a standard book by d'Endrody on training event horses and showjumpers (see Further Reading).

The obvious and appropriate question is: *'How do I come by such a state of balance?'* The answer is to ride horses on the lunge, on the flat, over poles and small jumps, down grids and jumping lanes, and over whatever obstacles you feel you can tackle – without reins or stirrups and sometimes with your eyes closed! This has been the proven method for generations, and boy does it work, but modern health and safety officers, at least in the UK, would probably have a fit over it.

In practice, you can, of course, do what you want on your own place and on your own horse and if you kit yourself out wisely (hard hat, body protector) and take it in very gradual stages with a like-minded teacher or an experienced friend on the ground, you will come on in leaps and bounds (no pun intended). The essential condition for acquiring a basic, moulding seat is to keep your buttocks and legs relaxed whilst learning to feel what your horse is doing underneath you, for if your muscles are contracted and at all tight your body cannot go with him softly and you cannot achieve the upright, deep (but light and soft), vertical seat which is the hallmark of classicism, balance and horse-friendly riding.

As your ability and technique improve, you can do this and also start introducing muscular tone (slight contraction) into your body to help you keep in position, move as little as required and also give your aids. Of course, if you really don't want to jump, then don't, but at least do pole work – and take it all as slowly as you need to in order to become proficient and confident.

## Rhythm

With the establishment of forwardness and balance comes rhythm. No horse can move with a good, regular beat if he is not swinging along and in balance. These qualities give him the feeling of security and you can then feel for his natural rhythm in each gait. A sluggish horse can improve no end if he is schooled to become forward and balanced and he will then produce a lovely, active rhythm which you may never have seen before.

A hot, sensitive horse prone to running on or skittering about can likewise calm down, relax and swing along in his own rhythm, which may previously have been obscured. It gives him a great sense of security, relief and enjoyment.

You can influence any horse by maintaining his rhythm with your seat. Some people have a great sense of rhythm and some do not, but being in close, relaxed contact with a horse can help you to develop it. So can playing music as you ride, of course, but you need to be careful to gear the beat to your horse and not vice versa in order to get the best out of him.

# STRAIGHTNESS

The general definition of straightness is that the horse's hind hooves follow exactly in the tracks of his fore hooves whether he is on a straight line or a curve. Some horses seem to have no problem with straightness and are naturally straight, whether mounted or dismounted, but others are naturally crooked. Given the choice, many carry their hindquarters to one favoured side, whichever rein they are on, and a few habitually go quarters-in or quarters-out on both reins.

Why is straightness so desired in riding horses? The reasons are that:

1. In a straight horse the hindquarters can function better and more directly in their role of pushing or propelling the horse's body forward in the chosen direction.
2. The weight distribution of the horse and (if ridden) his rider is more even, no part of the body bearing more or less weight and energetic force than it should.

For these reasons, it is understandable that a straight horse must be less prone to physical stress and strain than a crooked one; he can work more easily and presumably better and is easier and more comfortable to ride than if he were crooked. If he is straight on straight lines and curves, his lateral work will also be more accurate and, again, easier to accomplish; also halts will be straight and his rein-back should also be straight.

The fact that a horse is crooked by nature is no reason to leave him in this condition: he will certainly benefit from being worked to improve his straightness by developing his muscles evenly and having his natural weight distribution and action improved. He becomes lighter to ride because he is in better and more even balance, his self-control and 'self-function' improve, movements are easier to perform, he will be more willing in schooling and work because he feels more able and he will find it easier to maintain free, forward movement and impulsion. At a more advanced stage, true collection becomes possible – collecting a crooked horse is pretty much an impossibility.

## Assessing Horse and Rider for Straightness

Many riders cannot feel whether or not their horse is straight or crooked. This is usually because they are too tense in the seat and legs. Riding with relaxed seat and leg muscles, and stretching up from above the waist and dropping down from below the waist, so that your body has two independent halves, makes it much easier for you to feel straightness or crookedness. If your seat and leg muscles are tense, it is so much more difficult to feel what the horse is doing underneath you.

It is a good plan to watch your horse moving at liberty and study him closely to see whether his hind feet do, indeed, follow directly in the tracks of his forefeet or whether they deviate to one side or the other, or both. Most horses have a 'stiff' side and a 'soft' side. The muscles on the soft side are always a little shorter, more contracted, than those on the stiff side. The horse will find it easier to work on curves on his soft-side rein and vice versa, i.e. if he feels softer and easier on the right rein, his work on curves will be easier for both of you on that rein. However, you may have to be careful that the horse does not tend to 'curl in' on that rein, so you will still require prudent use of the correct aids.

You can also benefit from having a knowledgeable teacher or friend on the ground, assessing the movement of your horse when ridden, to tell you whether or not he is straight. If he is crooked, you need to know whether it is his natural crookedness or your own crookedness or otherwise faulty position in the saddle that is causing it. If there is any uncertainty about the cause, a really good rider should ride the horse, making no attempt to straighten him but sitting very centrally while the horse is assessed again. If the horse is now straight, then your position is the problem. If it is the rider's fault that the horse is crooked, the remedy is clearly to correct the rider with good instruction. If it is the horse, sensitive riding is needed to straighten him up gradually, and this may take a few months or maybe even a year or so depending on the extent of the problem.

A big advantage is being able to ride in a school with mirrors on at least one short and one long side, so that you can assess your horse and yourself as you ride.

Finally, remember that an uncomfortable saddle (especially one in poor condition) can be a cause of crookedness.

## Straightening the Crooked Horse

It will be necessary to work the horse, and ideally give him bodywork, to encourage the gradual freeing and stretching of the shorter muscles and tissues on his shorter, softer side (see preceding section). A physiotherapist, on referral by a veterinary surgeon, can be of great help in this, as can an equine massage therapist, an osteopath, a chiropractor or a shiatsu practitioner, depending on what the cause appears to be after veterinary diagnosis. It could be an injury which may, or may not, be causing actual pain. The injury may be old but could have resulted in shortened muscles which now work in a more restricted way, albeit painlessly. It is important to take advice, with a crooked horse, to determine the reason for his crookedness before starting on a remedial or schooling programme to straighten him up.

A horse who is just naturally crooked needs to be worked very correctly, gently and sensitively, on the ground and/or under saddle, on his stiff side to try to stretch the muscles on his soft side. Let his corners on this side be shallow and his curves and circles large and sweeping. If he feels awkward or starts to lean in on curves of a particular degree, you will know he is finding it difficult. For example, a 20 m circle may feel all right but one of 18 m may be just too tight for him, as yet. There is no point in trying to force him into a tighter curve (or into anything) as this can create other problems, both mental and physical, such as faulty, compensatory action which will stress other tissues, and dislike of work caused by discomfort, or even fear. You can help him with your own balance and aids (see Chapter 8).

Apart from ensuring that you yourself are straight in the saddle, when realigning the horse, always move the forehand in front of the hindquarters and not the other way round, even though you may think the latter is easier. Moving the forehand necessitates the horse taking his weight back on to his quarters to lighten the forehand and thus making it easier to move. If you use your leg to move his quarters, he will put weight forward on to his forehand in order to move them. This does not encourage or develop lightness.

As mentioned earlier, a simple aid to move the forehand over is simply to press the rein on the side to which he is inclined against his withers, or just in front of them, with a firm, intermittent pressure. If necessary, press on and off with your knuckles. So, if you are travelling on the centre line of a manège and the horse is travelling with his quarters to the left, bring his forehand to the left in front of them by pressing with your right rein or knuckles. An open rein on the other side supports your request for him to move his forehand over. A very simple version of this is to simply move both your hands sideways a little to the side to which you need to move the forehand. Once the forehand is in front of the quarters, you can ride back on to the centre line.

Exercises for improving straightness are:

- Shoulder-fore, shoulder-in and shoulder-out (to get control of the forehand and accustom the horse to bringing his weight on to his quarters and moving his forehand).
- Turns about the haunches or walk pirouettes (to bring weight on to the quarters and develop forehand mobility).
- Work along narrow corridors of poles on the ground.

Horses who are naturally crooked can still benefit from treatment from a professional bodyworker such as a massage or shiatsu therapist.

The end result of the horse's treatment and work and, where necessary, the correction of the rider, should be a horse easy to place anywhere you wish, once 'made' or schooled.

# CHAPTER 11

# What to Teach When

A lot of problems are caused to horse and rider by the latter's attempting to teach the various techniques and movements in the wrong order, so omitting basic schooling exercises and not giving the horse the foundation necessary to perform more advanced ones. The training progression outlined in this chapter is given for guidance. While it is pretty reliable, it should be remembered that horses differ in their inclinations, abilities and talents and not all horses can do everything an equestrian curriculum may set out, particularly at the more advanced end of schooling. Trainers schooling horses for entertainment such as display work usually understand this: they will give each horse very good basic training and, as he progresses, will find out what he is good at and likes doing, cultivate it and let it form part of the horse's repertoire.

Another viewpoint is that a trainer should develop and strengthen a horse's weak points and pay less attention to the good ones, which the horse will do well anyway. A lot depends on what you want your horse for but, as far as is reasonably possible, it is a good plan to create an all-round horse who can do most things – a sort of Jack of All Trades but Master of Two or Three. Cross-training, as it is now called, creates a versatile horse who has an interesting life, a supple body, a mind geared to investigating and learning new things and a confident, settled attitude to life.

Until about the middle of the last century, before the boom in competitive riding, a horse was not considered a made riding or saddle horse until he was capable of what many people now would consider advanced standards, but which were perfectly ordinary then. He had to be very obedient, well balanced and agile, back on his quarters, have comfortable, straight, even gaits, be forward and impulsive, be very light and capable of being ridden with one hand – the bridle hand, which is the left – so that the right was free for other things such as raising your hat to friends and acquaintances if you were a gentleman or waving to them if a lady, opening gates out riding or hunting, or tipping the person who opened them for you, and so on. The horse had to stand stock-still when told to and had not to move until the rider gave the aid. He needed to be capable of flying changes, lateral movements such as half-pass and full pass which only police, bull-fighting, high school and circus horses are now required to do, turns on a sixpence (about the size of a five-pence piece and, obviously, a figure of speech) and rein-back, all with ease and instant compliance. There had to be no question of his biting, kicking, napping, shying, bucking, rearing or bolting, or even 'getting strong'. (Plenty of horses did these things, of course, but they were not made horses.)

It has to be admitted that the massive majority of horses used for general pleasure riding today come nowhere near to this standard and are often not even particularly safe to ride. Surely, not schooling a horse to a standard at which he is safe under saddle is not horse-friendly. Unsafe horses are prone to injuries if they 'misbehave' whether in a school or out hacking, to being punished by ignorant riders who feel that the horse is to blame, and to being passed from owner to owner, often ending up being neglected, abandoned or put down. In the process, they can seriously injure people, cause accidents and generally be a major liability. Horses are flesh and blood, with minds of their own. Some may never be capable of being made safe but the massive majority could be improved tremendously by implementing a decent schooling programme.

The following plan will take your horse to an above-basic standard which will make him manoeuvrable and give him the habit of co-operation, so he will be safer than most today to ride in a school or out hacking. To develop and educate any horse, I believe you need:

1. The personal commitment to take it seriously and thus give the time and money necessary to it.
2. A capsule library of helpful books (see Further Reading) and the will to learn as much as you can.
3. A teacher/trainer who has your and your horse's interests at heart, the knowledge and skills to train both of you effectively and humanely, and an understanding of the inevitable problems which arise.

# SUGGESTED SCHOOLING SEQUENCE UNDER SADDLE

When carrying out the following exercises, always be mindful of the following:

- *At all times, concentrate on forwardness without nagging your horse.*
- *Maintain a comfortable contact for your horse, steady and neither loose nor hard.*
- Give plenty of rests on a completely loose rein.
- Keep it short and stay relaxed!

1. Walk on straight lines, but don't worry too much about actual straightness at this stage.
2. Walk on shallow curves, then 20 m circles, with slight inside flexion.
3. From walk, transitions to halt and to trot without resistance. Concentrate on standing still; don't worry about a square halt yet.
4. First two exercises in flowing, rhythmic trot.
5. Changes of rein with correct flexions (so you can just see the horse's inside eye) in walk and trot.
6. Introduce turn around the forehand (to gain control of quarters), few steps at first, gently.
7. Leg-yield in walk.
8. Introduce walking then trotting over poles, (adjusting the spacing as necessary) starting with one pole and never more than six when the horse is stronger.
9. Shoulder-fore in walk, then shoulder-in and shoulder-out.
10. Transition from trot to canter in a corner of the school.
11. Introduce small, single jumps from trot.
12. Introduce hacking in company of one or two bombproof, older horses.
13. Canter on straight lines in light seat, returning to trot before corner.
14. Transitions to trot on 20 m circle, with reasonably correct flexion and 'bend'.
15. Changes of rein, canter-trot-walk-trot-canter. Maintain light seat in canter.
16. Changes of rein, canter-trot-canter. Maintain light seat in canter, then normal seat.

17. Serpentines: 2-loop, then 3-loop in 20 x 40 m school, walk and trot.
18. Improve walk-halt transitions, work on square halt but do not nag horse.
19. Walk 15 m circles.
20. Trot 15 m circles.
21. Rein-back, only one step at first and immediately walk forward, relaxed, without the horse raising his head.
22. Some shortening and lengthening of stride in walk and trot, then canter.
23. Improved transitions up and down, without resistance and horse in good posture/outline for his level. (Downward transitions more difficult than upward.)
24. Start developing impulsion from forwardness.
25. Introduce canter poles, starting with one, up to six.
26. Canter 15 m circles.
27. Canter large serpentines, changing lead first through walk and trot, then just through trot.
28. Walk to canter.

Good 'straightness' on a bend. The horse is actually turning his head a little too much into the bend. The rider is 'pushing' him and guiding him round his circle by light, outside rein pressure against the left side of his neck rather than pulling him round with the inside rein – the latter being a very common fault. She could maintain this aid with the outside rein but just use a little more bit contact on that side to correct the head position. Note that the horse's hind feet are exactly following his forefeet on this curved track.

At all times, remember that horses will vary in their abilities to perform particular movements, but the above are the sorts of things that any sound, normally conformed horse can do and constitute an above-basic education to perhaps spur (sorry!) you on to higher things. The better you both are, the more you'll both enjoy your riding.

## POLE WORK AND JUMPING

Working horses over poles really makes them think and use themselves. It develops muscular pushing/lifting power and agility, improves flexibility of joints and gives them a bit of a challenge if you ride correctly and take it very gradually, starting with walking over just one pole.

An older horse being re-schooled may have had bad experiences with poles and jumps, so be prepared for him to either try to jump the poles (maybe even a line of six) or to dither or refuse. Your horse will probably want to lower his head to look at the poles so let him do so, keeping just a light contact. When he is familiar with them, you can ride him over them in a normal long-and-low posture (whatever his age or level of schooling) and progress to a normal riding posture. (Spacings which are *slightly* longer, rather than shorter, suit this posture best.) Do not tense up or become anxious about poles if you have never done them before. Stay relaxed in your seat and legs, control your upper body, have a light but guiding contact and ride positively forward without rushing, in your horse's normal rhythm. Look ahead to some marker, never down at the poles or at your horse. Do not accept a faulty posture from him (head up, back down, hind legs trailing) as this will do harm, not good. Establish a good gait and posture first, *then* present him at the poles. Aim to take off and land midway between poles so there is less chance of his treading on them and startling himself: if he does, however, it will teach him a lesson about placing his feet, but without harming him. Always use heavy, round poles which are easy to manoeuvre but should not hurt the horse if he does tread on them. (In the event of any repeated treading on poles, remember that correct footfalls are largely a result of a combination of correct distances between poles for the individual horse and good, 'forward' rhythm, so check these factors.)

## *Approximate Distances between Poles*

Horses vary, of course, in their natural and comfortable stride lengths, but the following are reasonable lengths for an average riding horse of around 16 hands. If his stride feels too tight or as though he is struggling to make the distance, lengthen or shorten the distance accordingly till you have it just right. (A perceptive and nimble helper on the ground is very useful!) Later, when he is used to pole work, you can adjust the distances to help him with shortening and lengthening of stride, if you so wish.

- A walk stride distance between two poles is about 0.75 m (2 ft 6 in), which is a short human stride or about three of your foot lengths. It may be a little longer for some horses.

- A trot stride distance between two poles is about 1.20 m (4 ft), which is a long human stride. (Again, maybe a little longer in some cases.)
- A canter stride distance between two poles is about 3.3 m (11 ft) which is about three comfortable human strides.

## Small Jumps

Small, single jumps are fun for most horses and do not challenge most riders. Make them cross-poles, at first, set at a very modest height and aim, in trot, straight at the crossed area, looking ahead at a marker.

### THE HORSE- AND RIDER-FRIENDLY JUMPING SEAT

You should not be too forward for any height of obstacle as this puts you out of balance and so can be dangerous. A very small jump does not warrant shortened stirrup leathers or a change in your basic position; just remain soft, stable and balanced.

If you aim for higher jumps, bear in mind that your horse *must* have the freedom of his head and neck to negotiate them freely, in natural balance and with enjoyment. Shorten your stirrups a couple of holes or so to a comfortable length and adopt a light or half seat, with your shoulders above or just behind your knees on a vertical line. Most of your horse's movement should be absorbed by your hip, knee and ankle joints.

Keep your back flat and, as your horse jumps, fold your upper body *down* (not forward) from your hip joints, as though you are trying to touch the crest of his neck with your breastbone, and push your seat *back*. This will enable you to fold down correctly, stay with (rather than in front of) his movement and jump in effortless, secure balance, allowing your horse to take you with him. Your lower legs stay down, with their joints soft, and your stirrup leathers vertical. Keep a straight line from your elbow, through your hand to your horse's mouth and allow your hands to follow your horse's mouth *downwards* in a diagonal line. They must remain independent, not touching your horse, to give him physical and psychological freedom to make his jumping effort without hindrance.

*Do not bend forward from your waist* as this will make you crouch, and do not throw your upper body forward up his neck (probably with your lower legs swinging back), as this is unbalanced and unsafe, despite the fact that many people do it. Certainly do not haul yourself up your horse's neck by the hands as he takes off, or thrust your hands up his neck towards his ears

An excellent way to acquire an independent seat when jumping, which is essential so that the rider can allow the horse complete freedom of his head and neck during the activity. Horse and rider could progress to a more difficult exercise by jumping down a grid of fences the same way.

and/or prop yourself with them on his neck. This completely blocks the essential forward and down movement of his head and neck so you are effectively stopping him jumping naturally and correctly to best effect.

## Grid Work

Grids of little jumps just high enough to require him to pop rather than step over them are an excellent way of making a horse strong, athletic and aware, provided you build up slowly and get your distances right. Recruit a friend to note your horse's comfortable non-jumping stride lengths (the distances you use for ground-poles are a guide) and his jumping stride lengths (that is, take-off to landing), placing markers on the ground where his leading leg lands. You can use poles raised to the lowest height on plastic jumping blocks and make a grid of, initially, two cross-poles, progressing to six when he is strong and experienced.

Initially, place two jumps so that he makes two non-jumping strides between them, then very gradually increase the number of jumps. Also, in time, reduce the distance between them to one non-jumping stride, and finally make them all jumping strides or bounces. A line of six bounce jumps takes some doing for the horse, requiring agility, fitness and strength, but it will improve all those things, as well.

You can encourage and help him by adopting the technique described on page 183: if in doubt, maintain a *light* but present contact for this athletic task. If he starts to rush, it can be a sign that he is not quite ready for the number of grid jumps you are asking for. Steady him tactfully and reduce the number of efforts in the grid until he will jump through it calmly.

This kind of jumping exercise, when built up gradually, is fun for horse and rider and is an excellent preparation for higher jumps and courses, depending on your ambitions.

## HACKING

If you live in a good hacking area, you are very fortunate, for hacking is a wonderful way for both of you to enjoy the countryside and to get to know each other in the varying situations you will meet when out and about. A lot of people do not hack out because of traffic problems but it is worth arranging to transport your horse to a decent area to enjoy a hack, maybe with friends.

Contrary to popular opinion, hacking is not for useless riders and ploddy horses. You need to be a good rider to enjoy and be safe on a hack, and your horse needs to be controllable, even when his eyes are out on stalks. Like any other activity with horses, you can help the situation by hacking in safe company to accustom your horse to things like traffic, farm machinery and activities, dumped rubbish, joggers, cyclists, walkers (with or without running, screaming children, or dogs, whether well-behaved or otherwise), before going it alone.

There is an excellent book, *Bombproof Your Horse,* listed in Further Reading to help you create a worldly-wise horse and it is fun doing the training, anyway.

Horse and rider putting their skills to good use on a 'happy hack'.

Physically, hacking gets your horse fit and you can do a good deal of schooling out hacking – but don't nag your horse or school all the time. A hack is a brilliant opportunity to let your horse really stride out on a long or loose rein in walk, and develop a ground-covering gait which will help his mental attitude, his fitness and his other gaits. The old standards for the three gaits out hacking were that a horse should 'walk fast, trot slow and canter in between', and this is really good advice.

Psychologically, hacking educates your horse like nothing else apart from hunting. There is no competitive pressure, the object being solely to enjoy yourselves and take advantage of the secondary benefits such as broadening your horse's mind and increasing his trust in you. As his general schooling improves, he will enjoy working correctly over all sorts of ground, maybe jumping little obstacles and ditches, doing hill work and, if you are fortunate enough to live near a beach, having a spin on the sands and walking in the sea (but watch the footing). The hacking will benefit his schooling and your riding (just as schooling will benefit your hacking) so, if you are keen on hacking, carry on and enjoy yourselves and, if you don't hack, make the effort to do so and add another dimension to your life with your horse.

# CHAPTER 12

# When Things Go Wrong

I am sure that very, very few horses present no problems at all to their riders or trainers, no matter how expert they are. Experienced people will know how to deal with most of the problems that do occur, but less experienced ones, whether amateur or professional, may be over-faced, worried or even scared when an animal as reactive and heavy as a horse, or even a pony, starts giving you problems.

The important attitude to have, at a time like that, is one of brutal realism tempered with positivity. If you really don't know what to do next, or you realize that the problem is proving too difficult for you, or the horse is just getting on top of you, and knows it – get help.

It is only common sense to learn as much as you can, both from books and in practice, but often you cannot beat a consultation, a training session or lessons with a professional trainer or competent amateur *who is on the same wavelength as you*. Part of your learning process is to get to know how people who are in the same discipline, or have the same interests as you, operate. Word of mouth is usually the recommended way of finding a teacher or trainer, but you need to be very familiar with their methods *yourself* to know whether you both feel the same about the general schooling process.

Try going to some competitions, training days or lecture-demonstrations where such people will be and watch them and, more to the point, the horses they ride and handle. If those horses look distressed in any way, appear as if being forced, are being defensive, or look as though they have been browbeaten and have given up, try to watch for a little longer and make an honest decision about whether you would be truly happy to put your horse in their hands.

If all you see are good things such as a firm but kind attitude, horses who have a secure, confident look about them (study their faces and heads in particular), methods which do not distress horses, a calm, strong way of dealing with any giving trouble and so on, maybe you have found your trainer.

It is so much wiser to seek suitable help than to press on out of pride and make a mess of things. It's also a lot safer.

## SOME COMMON PROBLEMS

### Inherited Problems

There are all sorts of problems that can arise with horses and most are the fault of a human in the horse's present or previous life. A previous owner may have done things very differently from how you do them and the horse may now be confused, he may have been badly or incorrectly treated or schooled and be showing the effects of that, or he may have undetected or poorly treated injuries which affect him.

If you suspect that the horse's previous owner simply rode and handled him differently from your preferred methods, try to find out exactly what words and techniques were used on the ground and in the saddle. (Whenever possible, it is a good idea to get this information when first viewing the horse prior to purchase.) This will at least give you a starting point from which to get the horse into your own ways. This, in itself, can be a learning process for you: you might learn a lot from the previous owner and conclude that their ways might be better than yours. Horses most certainly can be retrained to respond to different cues and do different jobs – but so can humans.

If the horse is exhibiting a particularly troublesome behaviour, again, try asking the previous owner, if possible, whether or not they ever experienced such incidents. Of course, you may get an honest answer, or you may not. Very often, if some kind of tricky behaviour has not been declared at the time of sale, all you will get is, 'Well, he never did that with me'. If you cannot get to the bottom of why he is doing it, this is one situation in which you may need expert help.

Generally, if the horse has developed bad habits in his way of going in a previous home, but is sound and has good conformation and action, re-schooling him correctly, absolutely consistently and patiently will put them right. Bad habits can be replaced by good ones, which will reliably become evident unless the original circumstances which caused the bad ones recur. As mentioned earlier, horses learn very quickly and make associations between circumstances and happenings and will not forget, but even so, stick to your good methods and your horse will respond much better and more quickly than previously and eventually the good practices will take precedence in his mind.

A crooked rider makes for an uncomfortable horse working under a handicap – literally.

## Newly Apparent Problems
### INJURIES

Injuries, whether new or newly apparent, are obviously a job in the first instance for your vet, but even an apparently serious injury may not mean the end of a horse's working life. It is worth remembering that, while a horse is recovering from a longer-term injury, this may be a good time to establish a strong personal bond with him (and minimize his boredom), or to allow him to relax into a new environment. Even if he does not recover fully, perhaps a sideways move to another job, or to a less demanding one, will place less stress on a weakened part and enable the horse to continue to be useful and still feel a part of things.

### 'TRYING YOU OUT'

Whether your horse is a youngster, or an older, green horse, good schooling methods should obviously be used but, even so, horses (being individuals) may come up with unexpected difficulties for no apparent reason. This is sometimes described as the horse 'trying you out'.

I know, and know of, several people who will say that horses do not have the mentality to 'try people out' and, to a large extent, I tend to agree. There are times, though, when it certainly *seems* like that and you may feel as though you are being put to the test. There is never anything to be gained by getting rough with horses in this situation. Stand back and try to assess when and under what circumstances the behaviour started and you may find your answer.

Quite often, a horse perceived as doing this is objecting for some perfectly reasonable cause, such as he is not feeling well, he is tired or not 'in the mood', he is in pain or discomfort somewhere, he does not understand what you want (or he knows that what you are asking causes him discomfort, or he is frightened of trying it) – or he just does not like you personally. Horses can 'do' better for some people than others, of course, and it can be a very individual thing. As mentioned at the start of this chapter, the answer is to find help. A 'second eye' on a problem often sees something we have missed or looks at it from a quite different viewpoint and comes up with an answer.

Some horses appear to be quite amenable so long as they are doing what they enjoy and can do well, but when you start to push them out of their comfort zone a bit, even if you don't realize it, the situation can change dramatically. There certainly are seemingly lazy horses and horses who just don't want to make an effort. Some people will say 'and why should they?' – a point I certainly understand. However, if we, in the horse world, are going to ride horses, we want a horse who will do what we want, unless we are acquiescent enough to accept a horse who will only do what he is prepared to do. As a freelance teacher, I have come across many such combinations.

If the horse does see you as 'weaker' than he is, it could simply be that he feels insecure in your company and is objecting in the only way he knows how. Most horses are not naturally confrontational, and a horse who is genuinely trying to dominate a human is probably rarer than we imagine. However, if the consensus of opinion is that a horse really is dominating you and getting the upper hand, maybe you could be more confident and firmer with him, if only for safety's sake? To help with this, you may wish to remind yourself that horses, quite naturally, need and respond to appropriate

Not seeing eye to eye can happen to anyone. In the massive majority of cases when problems arise, the fault lies with the rider. The answer is to revive that invaluable, old quality 'equestrian tact'. Remember that, being prey animals, many horses become worried easily and *will* defend themselves, however mildly. Probably we should back off, give the horse some breathing space and encourage him to calm down before trying again.

Problem obviously solved – horse and rider swinging along in a forward trot, tracking-up and in good posture, with active hind legs and quarters.

discipline (see Chapters 2 and 3) and refresh your understanding of the principles of praise and reward (discussed at various points including Chapters 1, 2, 5 and 8). Perhaps also consider some further training for yourself and having someone else school the horse for a while. A year or so on, all the problems might dissolve away and you will be glad you persevered. If not, you may have to decide whether the two of you are really suited (see Parting Company, below).

## PARTING COMPANY

As with people and other animals, some combinations of horses and owners are like magnets pushing each other the opposite way rather than attracting each other. Anyone with a feeling for horses will know (even if they don't want to admit it at first) when they and their horse should go their separate ways.

If, after taking all reasonable steps to establish a good relationship, it becomes clear that you and your horse cannot get on, do not seem to have any kind of connection and cannot see any hope of its happening in the future (in other words, are going nowhere together), it is better for both of you to part. It is best for you and, *if you make genuine efforts to find the right home for the horse*, better for him, too.

We don't like admitting defeat, (if we see it that way), but time and life are precious, and horses have even shorter lives than people. New partners for both of you could at least give you the chance to make the best of what time you have and maybe find the horse-human relationship of a lifetime.

## Problems of Management

It has to be said that the likelihood of encountering the problems addressed here can be reduced by a combination of common sense and planning. However, we all misread situations from time to time and, if we have ambitions for our horses, it is easy enough to get a little carried away when things seem to be going well. Hopefully, the topics discussed here will serve as reminders that we should always retain an element of caution as we progress in our partnerships with our horses.

### TRAINING PLATEAUX

Quite often, you can ride and school a horse for some time with steady improvement, and then find that you are getting nowhere further. The horse has 'flattened out' in his training and you don't know what to do next. I find that the best course of action is usually to back off a bit. Give him a rest from that particular work, or a complete holiday, for a few weeks or even months. Almost always, when you return to schooling, the horse starts to improve again. Horses never forget, so you will not have to start schooling all over again. A short period refreshing your previous work is enough, and then you can gently introduce more new tasks, if that is your plan.

The brain and the body can only cope with so much. It could be that, although he hasn't shown it, or you haven't spotted it, you have been moving on a little too fast for him. A break enables the brain to 'process' things and, when you come back to them after a decent break, they are established and the horse does not have a problem learning something else. This happens in human education, as well, and is a phenomenon educationists have recognized for some time.

## STALENESS

We often hear of horses in hard work going 'over the top'. The human version of it is known as being 'burnt out'. The horse's work deteriorates, as does his well-being and attitude. Again, the answer is a break for a few weeks or months to enable the mind and body to be restored, relaxed and refreshed.

The problem can be avoided to some extent by keeping the horse on as natural a daily regime as is possible. Many people still do not believe in turning out hard-working horses (or even those who do not work particularly hard but are used for some milder form of work, usually competitive). Such people have all sorts of reasons for denying their horse a taste of their natural lifestyle and food, but they are not always genuine or reasonable. If grass 'will make a horse ill', such as if he is allergic to grass or easily gets laminitis, then there is a reason for having it *restricted* but I do not think it fair treatment to deny horses grass as a matter of course, even though some of the 'best' establishments do it.

Good hay or haylage are obviously welcome, but grazing has psychological benefits as well as satisfying the horse's need to eat almost constantly. Horses grazing move about slowly, swinging their heads from side to side as they crop the grass, and this seems to be an inbuilt need for them. It certainly has a wonderfully calming effect on them. Even an hour or two a day on most days will help to satisfy their needs and keep them fresher.

Freedom on a surfaced area is obviously second best to turnout, but better than nothing. However, some horses will not settle if they have no hay or water available, even when in company, so it's best to put them out, not only with friends, but also with hay and water. In my experience they often play about, then come for a snack, play a bit more, and so on. This is much better than only being exercised by people.

Another reason given for not giving horses freedom is that they might injure themselves. So they might, but they can do this during work and even in the stable. It is unreasonable to deny them liberty and goes against one of the Five Freedoms (animal care guidelines), which states that they must be allowed freedom to express most acts of normal behaviour by providing sufficient space for this, proper facilities and company of their own kind.

The better horses are treated – in their terms, not merely ours – generally the more content, enthusiastic and problem-free they stay. A relatively natural life is the answer.

# MAINTAINING YOUR HORSE'S SPIRIT

Spirit may be somewhat indefinable but it is an important part of humans' and horses' states of being. I call maintaining a horse's spirit allowing him to be himself and enjoy his life, with his own unique personality, and not to use 'brain-washing', bullying and mentally abusive riding and schooling techniques even if they are not physically painful – and those that are, must be absolutely out.

A horse with his spirit intact but with consideration (yes, consideration) for people is a joy to be with. Some horses are naturally well-mannered equine ladies and gentlemen. Some learn manners and a few will be forever morons, but most have something to offer us if we treat them fairly. How can anyone teach a horse to look after a novice rider, for instance, particularly when that same horse will behave completely differently with an experienced one? I cannot see that it is possible. This has to come from the horse's spirit.

I had an Anglo-Arab who always used to stand aside and let me go through doors and gateways first, and I certainly never taught him this. Once, when we both dived towards the stable door at the same time to see who had just arrived in the yard, and knocked into each other, I went flying. The look on his face as he stepped back was one of horror. I know some people who would have hit him for this – a sure-fire way of destroying a horse's spirit. I stroked him and apologized to him for getting in his way and he blew gently in my face: incident over.

To my mind, friends should always be ready to forgive small misunder-standings, regardless of who (if anyone) is 'at fault'. Sometimes, we make mistakes – sometimes, our horses do. Let's not sully our friendly relation-ships with our horses by being too eager to excuse our own failings, and too ready to react to theirs.

# Further Reading

The books on this list are those I suggest as an all-round 'capsule' library to cater for the schooling, riding, care and management of riding horses, whatever work they do. Some of them are out of print but well worth searching for through second-hand dealers or online.

Belasik, Paul, *A Search for Collection*, J.A. Allen (London) 2009

Bishop, Ruth, *The Horse Nutrition Bible*, David & Charles (Newton Abbot) 2003.

Budiansky, Stephen, *The Nature of Horses*, Weidenfeld & Nicholson (London) 1997.

De la Guérinière, François Robichon, *School of Horsemanship*, J.A. Allen (London) 1994.

d'Endrody, Lt. Col. A.L., *Give Your Horse a Chance: The Training of Horse & Rider for Three-Day Eventing and Show Jumping*, J.A. Allen (London) 1959.

Devereux, Sue, *The Veterinary Care of the Horse*, J.A. Allen (London) 2006.

Fisher, Sarah, *Know Your Horse Inside Out*, David & Charles (Newton Abbot) 2006.

Gray, Peter, MVB, MRCVS, *Essential Care of the Ridden Horse*, David & Charles (Newton Abbot) 2002.

Hannay, Pamela, *Shiatsu Therapy for Horses*, J.A. Allen (London) 2002.

Heuschmann, Dr. Gerd, *Tug Of War: Classical Versus 'Modern' Dressage*, J.A. Allen (London) 2007.

Kiley-Worthington, Marthe, *Horse Watch: What it is to be Equine*, J.A. Allen (London) 2005 and any other titles by this author.

Loch, Sylvia, *Invisible Riding: the secret of balance for you and your horse*, D.J. Murphy (Publishers) Ltd. (Haslemere) and any other titles by this author.

McBane, Susan, *From Warming Up to Cooling Down*, J.A. Allen (London) 2007.
— *Revolutionize Your Riding*, David & Charles (Newton Abbot) 2008.

McLean, Andrew, *The Truth About Horses: A guide to understanding and training your horse*, David & Charles (Newton Abbot) 2003.

Nelson, Hilda, *Alexis-Francois l'Hotte: The Quest for Lightness in Equitation*, J.A. Allen (London) 1997.

Pelicano, Rick, *Bombproof Your Horse*, J.A. Allen (London) 2004.

Skipper, Lesley, *Inside Your Horse's Mind: A Study of Equine Intelligence and Human Prejudice*, J.A. Allen (London) 1999 and any other titles by this author.

Stanier, Sylvia, L.V.O., *The Art of Long Reining*, J.A. Allen (London) 1995.
— *The Art of Lungeing*, J.A. Allen (London) 1993.

Podhajsky, Alois, *The Complete Training of Horse and Rider*, The Sportsman's Press (London) 1997 and other editions.

Wilson, Anne, *Top Horse Training Methods Explored*, David & Charles (Newton Abbot) 2004.

# Index

abuse 23, 80–1, 110, **124**, 128–9, 156–7
action 32–3, 34
  'athletic' 39
  'true' 32, 36–7
adaptability, horses' 44, 45
aerobic respiration 153
'aged' horse 52
age of horse
  at which to start training 52–3, 59–60
  length of working life 52
aids
  artificial 83–4, 107–9
  breathing 107
  defined 82
  improving response to 146–7
  legs 23, 78, 96–7, 146–7, 165–6
  natural 83, 107
  reins/bit 97–9, **98**
  resistance to 17, 79, 148–9
  seat/weight 103–6
  strength of 16–17
  sustained pressure 23, 67–8
  teaching/training young horses 69–71
  voice 53–4, 64–5, 84–5, 138
  *see also* contact
all-rounders 41
ankle joint 86
anxiety, in horse 48–9
Arab horses 38, 40, 162
associations 22, 65–6, 69
  negative 20
  teaching of aids 69–71

attitudes, rider's 73–4

backing (starting) 69–71
  of older horse 59–60
back-to-front riding 156, 167
bad experiences 20
ballroom dancing 82–3
'banking' (turns/circles) 104
behaviour, natural 43, 61–3, **62**
'behind the bit' 40, 101, 102, **128**, 161–2
belly, sagging 28
bit
  abusive use 17, 80–1, **124**
  aids 97–8
  choice of 123–4
  curb 99–100, 125, 126
  fitting 121, 125–6
  flavoured 22, 124
  mouthpiece thickness 124
  problems/resistance 49, 101–2
  snaffle 124–5
bitless bridle 126–7
bits, gags 100, 102
body language
  horses' perception of 43
  understanding horses' 48–50
  use in lungeing 137–8
body rope 140–1
body wrap 141
bone 151
boots 57, 132–3
brain, horse's 18–19, 151
breastbone 28
breathing, rider's 107

breeds of horse/pony 16, **17**, 23–4
bridle
  bitless 126–7
  double 99–100, 125, 126
  fitting of 23, 121–2
  riding without **74**
bridoon rein 99
browband 121, 122
brushing 33
bucking 23, 171

cadence 38
calmness 45, 168–71
cannon bones 38
canter
  footfall sequence 35
  quality 37–8
  rider's seat 91–3
  stride length 183
cartilage 151
Chambon 127, 133, 139
change, horses' adaptability to 44
circles, *see* curves and circles
close-contact saddle 114
collection 166–7, 174
colts 60
compensatory movement 24
competition, equestrian 53, 72–3, 76
concentration, horses' 47
confidence, horses' 80, 168–9
conformation 24–34
  feet 33–4
  forelimbs 29, 30–1, **31**, 38
  head and neck 25, 26–7, 162
  hind limbs 31–3

hindquarters 28, 41
   related to horse's 'job' 41–2
   symmetry 24–6
   trunk 27–8
contact 17, 80–1, 100–2
   stable 160–1
   sustained/strong 23, 67–8, 156–7
   weight/strength of 100–1
correction 53–4, 65, 109–10
crookedness, *see* straightness
cross-training 24, 178
croup-high horse 27
curb bit/bridle 99–100, 125, 126
curves and circles
   rein aids 98–9, **98**
   riders' seat and weight 92, 104–6,
     107
   straightness 175–7, 181

'daisy-cutting' 38
dancing, comparison with riding 82–3
de Gogue 127
discipline 53
domestication of horses 72
dominant horse 77–8, 190–1
double bridle 99–100, 125, 126
draw reins 127
dressage girth 118
dressage horse 39, 41
dressage saddle 115

ears, horses' 49
elbows, horses' 27, 37
endurance horse 42
engagement 30, 155–61, 163
entire horse 60
eyes, horses' 49
eyesight, horses' 21

facial expression, horses' 48–9, 123–4
fear, in horse 46, 49, 102, 147–8
feeding 171
feet, conformation 33–4
Fisher, Sarah 140
Five Freedoms 193
flexion, teaching 159–60
foals 53, 62
   handling 54–6
food rewards 22, 64
foot-pastern axis 31, 33–4

forehand, on the 164
forelimbs, conformation 29, 30–1,
   **31**, 38
forward aids 93–4
   resistance to 79, 148–9
   teaching and improving response
     to 78, 145–7
forward, definition of 144–5
forwardness 171–4
   resistance to 171

gag bits/bridles 100, 102
gaits
   'athletic' 39
   description of 34–6
   qualities of 36–41
gallop 35
gelding, age of 60
girth 117–18
   position of **113**, 119
   tightening 120
girth (conformation) 28
glycogen 153
grazing (turnout) 171, 193
grid work 184–5
groundwork
   benefits of **130**, 131
   jaw flexions 159–60
   methods 130–1
   young horses 56–9
   *see also* long-reining; lungeing

habits, horses' learning of 63–4, 83
habituation, to whip 81
hacking 185–6
halting, use of seat 93
hands 99–100, 123
head, rider's 86
head-carriage 39–40
   behind the vertical 40, 101, 102,
     **128**, 161–2
   forced/restricted 26, 67–8, 127–9,
     **128**, 156–7
   natural 26–7, 40
   young horse 58–9
headpiece, bridle 121
hearing, horses' 21
height of horse 41, 42
herd life 43, 61–3, **62**
hind limbs, conformation 31–3

hindquarters
   conformation 28, 41
   engagement 155–6, 163
   muscular development 150, 161
hip joint, horses' 30
hocks 31–2
horse-friendly riding, aims of 13–14
horsemanship, defined 75–6
horses' qualities 15–16
   challenging 19–21
   positive 16–19
horse–rider relationship 43, 73,
   169–71, 194
'hyperflexion' 161–2

Iberian horses 40, 162
impulsion 144, 163–6
   preparation for 163
   *versus* speed 101, 163–4
injuries 29, 59, 176, 189
inside rein aids 98–9, **98**
instincts **18**, 20–1, 147–8
integrity, rider 76
intelligence, horses' 18–19, 45

judges 12
jumping 36, 181–5
   and conformation 41–2
   grid work 184–5
   horses' natural ability 19, **19**
   horses' vision for 21
   loose 38, 143
   rider's seat 87–8, 94–5, 183–4
   without a bridle **74**
   youngsters 53, 57
jumping saddle **113**, 114

keen horses 78–9, 97
knowledge, rider/owner 74
*Know Your Horse Inside Out* (Fisher)
   140

lactic acid 153
laminitis 34
lateral work 106, 177
lazy horses 78
lead, for young horses **69**
leading in hand **130**
   foal 54–5
learning 18–19, 109

associations 20, 22, 65–6, 69–71
bad habits 63–4
horses' capacity for 44–6
interactions with humans 63–4
in natural environment 61–3
leather care 112
leg aids 96–7
asking for impulsion 165–6
improving response to 78, 146–7
sustained pressure 23, 68
leg protection 57, 132–3
legs, position of rider's 86, 87, 88, 90
leg-yield 106
lengthening stride 163
L'Hotte, General Alexis-François 168,
169, 171, 172
ligaments 151
limbs, conformation 29–33
livery yard, change of 44
long and low **136**, 157–61
long-reining 69, 132
equipment 132–4
procedure 134–5
two-year-old 57
loose schooling 141–3
lumbo-sacral joint 30, 37
lungeing 135
aims of 138–9
equipment 136–7
of rider 75, 88–9
procedure 137–40
re-schooling lazy horse 78
side-reins 129, 139
young horses 57–8
lungeing cavesson 57, 70
lunge whip 78, 136–7, 147

'made' horse, requirements of 178–9
management 52, 192–4
manners, horses' 194
memory, horses' 19–20, 43–4
mental communication 106–7
mind maps 43–4
mouth 50
abuse of 17, 80–1, **124**
excessive salivation 49
problems with 49, 101–2
relaxed/happy horse 50
sensitivity 16–17
mouthpiece, bit 22, 124

movement, compensatory 24
muscles 152–5
development 24–5
functioning of 152–4
hindquarters 150, 161, 163
rest and relaxation 154
'ring' of 154–5
mutual grooming 66
myoglobin 153

name, use of horse's 85
napping **18**, 43
'natural horsemanship' 130
navicular disease 34
neck
conformation 25, 26–7, 162
restriction of 67–8, 127–9, **128**,
156–7
nerves 152
noseband 120, 121
'crank' 121
fitting 121, 122, 158
nostrils 49, 50
numnahs 116–17, **117**

Oliveira, Nuno 167
onagers 18
outline 154–5
and conformation 162
forced/restricted 67–8, 127–9,
**128**, 156–7
'long-and-low' **136**, 157–61
on lunge 139
overbent 101, 102, **128**, 161–2
overtrack 37
owner, attitudes 73–4
oxygen, muscles 153

paces, see action; gaits
pain 45, 102, 112
panel (saddle) 113, 116
panic 147–8
pasterns 31
perception, horses' ability 43, 62
personality types (horse) 76–80
photographing horses/ponies 25–6
point straps 120
poles, distances between 182–3
pole work 161, 181–3
posture (horse's) 154–5

defensive/concave 158, 159–60
long-and-low **136**, 157–61
over poles 161, 182
'ring of muscles' 154–5, 162
see also head-carriage
posture (rider's) 75, 82, 83
see also seat
power, developing 163
praise and reward 54, 64–5, 109, 145
predators 43, 61, 64
presence 41
pressure, response to 66–8, **66**, 146–7
problems, see training problems
psychology, equine 42–7
pullers 102–3

Questions Équestres (L'Hotte) 168

racing 53, 59
reasoning powers, horses' 46
rein aids 97–9, **98**, 102
see also contact
rein-back 36, 138
reins, handling 99–100
relationship, see horse–rider
relationship
re-schooling 182, 188–9
lazy horse 78
reticent horse 77
rewards 22, 54, 64–5, 109
rhythm 173–4
ribcage, horses' 28
Ride From the Heart (Rolfe) 107
rider
attitudes 73–4
balance 172–3
horse-friendly 50–1
posture 75, 82, 83
skill/technique 75
see also seat
'ring of muscles' 154–5, 162
Rolfe, Jenny 107
roller, driving 132
running reins 127

sacro-iliac joint 152
sacrum 152
saddle 114–16
dressage 115
fitting 23, 112–14, 175

jumping type **113**, 114
point straps 120
positioning 118–20
treeless 116
use when long-reining 134
VSD 115
saddle pads 116–17, **117**
saddling, problems with 64
safety 179
salivation, excessive 22, 49, 123
schooling programme 179–81
schooling sessions, length 47, 155
seat 85–94
balance 172–3
canter 91–2
'classical' 86–8
developing independence 75,
88–9
jumping and fast work 87–8,
94–5, 183–4
rising trot 91
sitting trot 90–1
straightness 103, 175
transitions 93–4
*see also* posture (rider's)
selling horse 191–2
senses, horses 21–3
sensitive ('hot') horses 78–9, 97
sensitivity, horses' 16–17
shoulder-fore 163
shoulder-in 163
shoulders
horses' 27, 31
rider's 87
showing classes 25, 58
show saddle 114
side-reins 129, **129**, 133, 139
skeleton 151–2
smell, horses' sense 21–2
snaffle bridle 99
sore ('bucked') shins 59
speed 17–18, 42, 145
controlling 78–9
*versus* impulsion 101, 163–4
speedicutting 33
spine 151–2
spirit, horses' 194
spooking 170–1
spurs 23, 108–9
staleness, horse 193

stamina, horses' 42
standing, training horse 65
Stanier, Sylvia 135
stirrup bars **113**, 114
stirrup leathers, length 90
stirrups 118
stirrup treads 118
straightness
exercises for 177
horse 174–7, 181
rider 103, 175
stride, length 37
survival instincts **18**, 20–1
symmetry (of horse) 24–6

tack
care of 112
checking 111
choosing and fitting 23, 111–12
*see also items of tack*
tail 28, 49, 50
taste, horses' sense of 22
teacher/trainer 129, 179, 187–8
teeth, horses' 49, 101
Tellington Touch Equine Awareness
Method 131, 140–1
temperament of horse 42, 45
tendons 152
tension, in horse 48–9
Thoroughbreds 38, 40, 59, 162
throat, conformation 27, 166
throatlatch 122
timid horse 77
tongue clicking 147
touch, sense of 23
training aids 127–9
training methods 11–12
causing pain/fear 45–6
natural horsemanship 130
Tellington Touch 131, 140–1
training plateaux 192
training problems 187–91
training schedules 179–81
five-year-olds 58–9
foals 54–6
four-year-olds 58
three-year-olds 57–8
two-year-olds 56–7
yearlings 56
transitions 93

treeless saddles 116
trot
footfall sequence 35
quality of 37
rider's seat 90–1
stride distances 183
trust 80–1
'trying you out' 189–91
turnout (grazing) 171, 193

uncooperative horse **18**, 79

'vertebral bow' 157–8
vision, horses' 21
visual communication 106–7
voice aids 53–4, 64–5, 69, 84–5
correction 53, 65, 109
flexions 159
lungeing 138
praise 53, 64–5

walk
footfall sequence 34–5
quality 37
stride distance 182
Warmbloods 162
warming-up **169**
weaning 56
weight aids 92, 103–6
welfare of horse 193
*see also* abuse
whip 23, 107–8
abuse of 110
habituation to 81
jumping 108
long-reining 133, 135
lungeing 136–7, 147
white wand 140
willing horse 80
withers 27
working-in 170

yearlings 56
young horses
age at which to start work 52–3,
59–60
backing/starting 69–71
lungeing 57–8
*see also under* training schedules